The Te

Commandments

I.   I *am* the LORD your God, who brought you out of the land of Egypt, out of the house of bondage. You shall have no other gods before Me.

II.   You shall not make for yourself a carved image, or any likeness of *anything* that *is* in heaven above, or that *is* in the earth beneath, or that *is* in the water under the earth; you shall not bow down to them nor serve them. For I, the LORD your God, *am* a jealous God, visiting the iniquity of the fathers on the children to the third and fourth *generations* of those who hate Me, but showing mercy to thousands, to those who love Me and keep My commandments.

III.   You shall not take the name of the LORD your God in vain, for the LORD will not hold *him* guiltless who takes His name in vain.

IV.   Remember the Sabbath day, to keep it holy. Six days you shall labor and do all your work, but the seventh day *is* the Sabbath of the LORD your God. *In it* you shall do no work: you, nor your son, nor your daughter, nor your male servant, nor your female servant, nor your cattle, nor your stranger who *is* within your gates. For *in* six days the LORD made the heavens and the earth, the sea, and all that *is* in them, and rested the seventh day. Therefore the LORD blessed the Sabbath day and hallowed it.

V.   Honor your father and your mother, that your days may be long upon the land which the LORD your God is giving you.

VI.   You shall not murder.

VII.   You shall not commit adultery.

VIII.   You shall not steal.

IX.   You shall not bear false witness against your neighbor.

X.   You shall not covet your neighbor's house; you shall not covet your neighbor's wife, nor his male servant, nor his female servant, nor his ox, nor his donkey, nor anything that *is* your neighbor's.

Exodus 20:2-17

THE
ANTICHRIST
AGENDA
TEN COMMANDMENTS TWICE REMOVED

DANNY SHELTON
SHELLEY J. QUINN

The Antichrist Agenda - Ten Commandments Twice Removed

This edition published 2004

Cover Photos by John Lomacang
Cover Design by John Lomacang

Published by DLS Publishing, Inc.
Printed by Remnant Publications, Inc.
Printed in the United States of America

ISBN 0-9720888-3-0

Scripture quotations used in the book are from the following sources:

Unless other noted, all Scripture quotations are taken from the New King James Version. Copyright © 1982 by Thomas Nelson, Inc. Used by permission.

Scripture quotations marked "NASB" are taken from the New American Standard Bible. Copyright © 1960, 1962, 1963, 1968, 1971, 1972, 1973, 1975, 1977, 1995 by the Lockman Foundation. Used by permission.

Scripture quotations marked "Amp" are taken from the Amplified Bible. Copyright © 1954, 1958, 1962, 1964, 1965, 1987 by The Lockman Foundation. Used by permission.

Scripture quotation marked "KJV" are taken from The Authorized King James Version of the Bible.

We dedicate this book to
seekers of the Truth

The coming of the *lawless one*
is according to the working of Satan,
with all power, signs, and lying wonders,
and with all unrighteous deception
among those who perish, because
they did not receive the love of the truth,
that they might be saved.
2 Thessalonians 2:9-10

Contents

Introduction

"Do you have this teaching in a book?"

His question caught me off guard. I usually sense who receives a blessing by the Bible messages I speak. This revival had been a good series. God was touching many hearts. I just didn't think this man's was one of them.

The previous evening, he had appeared agitated as I taught. When greeting him earlier on this day, his response had been—*well*—gruff.

"Do you have this teaching in a book?" When I replied *no*, he looked me straight in the eye and said, "That's a sin!"

I like people who don't pussyfoot around. They stir things up—spur you into action. Reflecting on his comment, I recognized it came as direction from the Lord.

The revival *theme* had been "The Foundation of Love." During the final meeting, the Holy Spirit impressed me to share a teaching I didn't plan to deliver—the difference between the Old and New Covenants.

On every occasion when I have shared my testimony of how the Lord led me through a study on His covenants to teach me the truth of His "Law of Love," people approach me with appeals to write it in a book. I had planned to do that—*some day*—but I had already decided my next book topic.

Still, I prayed about this new sense of direction. Suddenly, I was persuaded my procrastination was a sin. It *was* time to put this teaching in a book. Recognizing God's timing, I told my husband J.D. He would hold me accountable for completing the assignment.

Within days, we made a trip to the world headquarters of Three Angel's Broadcasting Network (3ABN). On the first day of our visit, Danny Shelton—the ministry's President—handed me a manuscript, *The Ten Commandments Twice Removed.*

"Could you please read this? I'd like your opinion. The publishers are ready for it, but if you have any suggestions or comments, feel free to mark this copy."

I glanced at the table of contents and inwardly cringed. *This is my book, Lord! The assignment I just accepted from you. Why would You give me a task that has already been accomplished?*

Reading the manuscript, I was amazed at how similar our teachings would be. Yet, I held out hope there could be room for two books. Mine would be sufficiently different. But God had another plan.

I didn't mention to Danny I was thinking of writing a book with this content, or that I was disappointed he beat me to the finish line. Later in the week, I suggested some changes for his opening chapter and offered to rewrite it.

When he read the revised chapter he asked, "How would you like to rewrite the whole book?"

Without hesitation, I agreed. Once the task was underway, the Lord convicted me to include the teachings that I selfishly clung to—wanting to reserve them for *my* book. I know any teachings that God gives me are His, *not mine.* I repented and determined to lay these on the altar for God's glory.

"God will bless you for this," J.D. said. "It's not about who gets credit. It's about presenting this truth the best you can. The book could be around a lot longer than either of you, and it can be life-changing to a lot of people."

When I first accepted this proposal, I expected no recognition other than heartfelt thanks for my efforts. This was a labor of love for God. Still, I confess, I did struggle briefly a couple of times. "Self" reared its ugly head—desiring credit for the teachings God had given me. Earnest prayer beat it back down.

A few weeks later, I returned to 3ABN. I had discussed with Danny some changes to the first few chapters, but had not yet shown him any more writings. The Lord really caught me off guard when Danny said—

"Shelley, just add your name as co-author. This is going to be as much your book as it is mine."

"Thank you," I muttered, without further comment—extremely unusual for me. But inwardly, I was rejoicing in the Lord's graciousness. God had raised my sacrifice from the altar.

God's ways are higher than our ways. His timing is always perfect! He laid the assignment on two of His children's hearts to co-author this book for His glory. God knew that both of us would bring a unique frame of reference to this—His book—that the other hadn't considered.

Danny grew up in these Bible teachings. My Christian experience was just the opposite. Although I was a serious student of Scripture and worked in part-time ministry, I had accepted several popular doctrines without thoroughly researching them. I was oblivious—even resistant—to these Bible truths until the Lord got my attention, at the dawning of my fifties, and taught me a new manner of in-depth Word study.

God entrusted this project to two people, coming from different perspectives. And He worked in each of us to make us willing to cooperate for His glory.

We have written *The Antichrist Agenda* to erase some popular errors the Christian community promotes today. As co-authors, it was important to both of us that the material we presented would be Bible-based.

To put an end to falsities, we felt it was imperative to present sufficient scriptural support. So, much of our book is really a well-organized Bible study. Although this is not a *light* read, our hope is that we have presented these truths in a logical sequence that you will find to be a *clear* and *compelling* read.

As with most books by co-authors, ours is written in the voice of only one. I chose to write in the first-person as if Danny were speaking. After all, he completed his manuscript before I had ever written a line.

My prayer is that God will anoint your mind and the Holy Spirit will be your Teacher. He can reveal truths beyond what is written here. I pray the Lord will use our book as a tool in His hands to make you hunger and thirst for more of His absolute truth.

To compile God's glorious teachings and present them in my own style of writing always leaves me feeling inadequate. But, I will say this in all humility—I wish someone had put a book like this in my hands forty years ago, regardless of how it read. My life history could have been rewritten.

What do I mean? God changed my life in the year 2000 when He led me through months of exhaustive Bible study. He taught me the truth of His Covenants and the Ten Commandments, His Law of Love.

From this, I learned how to depend totally on God—relying on Him for sanctification by faith. *Salvation by grace* and *righteousness by faith* became more than doctrines to me. God breathed life into these principles and they became mine through experience. Perhaps the most outstanding lesson I learned is that obedience is the pathway to His blessings.

I pray your experience is the same with our loving Savior.

Shelley J. Quinn

1

Twice Removed

Whose agenda are we following? With prayer prohibited in public schools, Nativity scenes banned from public properties, and the Ten Commandments forcibly removed from government institutions, it makes me wonder.

As I've watched the news over the last several years, it has become obvious to me that I'm not the only concerned Christian in America.

In the past, people of faith—not wanting to be branded lunatics—merely whispered, *There's a hidden agenda to remove God from our government.* But the picture has changed. The agenda doesn't seem quite so hidden now. The recent purging of the Ten Commandments from public institutions aroused a passionate response from many groups.

Consider the outcry in the case of former Alabama Supreme Court Justice Roy Moore, when defenders rushed to support the display of the Commandments monument. Today we hear religious leaders, laymen, and concerned individuals sounding the alarm. In my own home area, thousands of Christians are now displaying Ten Commandment replicas on their lawns.

Why? We have witnessed the grim results of our silence—

the ripple effect reaped from not standing in support of God's Word. Over the past hundred years, government leaders and atheistic special interest groups have accelerated the attack against the Bible.

For instance, our public schools now teach the *theory* of evolution as absolute *truth*. That would either amuse or alarm Darwin, the author of evolution theory. It's been reported he disclaimed much of his supposition in his later years.

Yet, no alternative to Darwin's speculation is suggested to students in public institutions. Teachers dare not to breathe a word of the biblical account and supporting evidence of a loving God with absolute creative power. What the majority of "Bible believers" accept as *truth,* our government declares *taboo*.

Does the banning of all representations of Bible truth convey that the United States government has clumped our foundational beliefs within the category of "theory"? Are life decisions now to be based on "political correctness" alone? What has happened since our nation quit relying on the supreme authority of God's Word?

For one thing, disregard for the Ten Commandments has fostered an acceptance of moral decay in our society. What was once spurned as *sin* is now considered *choice*. The Bible warns in Romans 6:23, "For the wages of sin is death."

What intellectually honest person can deny the consequences of sin today? Just consider the abortions and sexually transmitted diseases—spawned by promiscuous sexual behavior among heterosexuals, and the politics of promoting the homosexual lifestyle—that have resulted in hundreds of thousands of needless deaths.

Contempt for God's commandments is flagrant within the entertainment industry. Gone are the days of *I Love Lucy* and *Leave It to Beaver.* Sitcoms scoff at "old fashioned" morals. Dramas mock God at every turn.

As pleasure-seeking sin is more widely promoted, self-centered indulgence soars. Sex, pornography, violence and crime have become the accepted norm in movies, music, television, and the internet.

Pummeled with immoral images, the youth of America suffer. The assault on American values has advanced teenage pregnancies, suicides, illegal drug trafficking, school violence, and killing sprees by acne-faced kids.

Removing the Ten Commandments from public schools had repercussions beyond our stifled Christian concerns. Where there is no moral law, there is no law of decency to break. People are free to function without restraints.

Isn't it time to restore moral values in America? Don't you think the dividing line between right and wrong begs to be defined?

Sin must be defined for us to recognize we're trapped in its snare. God gave us a clear definition of sin in His Ten Commandments. Without this, people can't recognize their pitiful condition or their need for a Savior.

The searchlight of God's Word must shine into our moral darkness before we seek a solution from a loving God. What else would motivate us to turn to Christ in sincere repentance and accept Him as Savior?

When the brilliance of His light bursts into our lives, we confess our sins to Him. Gaining a fresh start, we rejoice in assurance that God is faithful to forgive us our sins and cleanse us from all unrighteousness (1 Jn 1:9).

The results? Gone are the guilt and condemnation that harbored hopelessness. By the power of the Holy Spirit, we gain victory over sin. As Christ promised, we begin to experience life "more abundantly" (Jn 10:10).

But where there is no recognition of sin, there is no repentance and no forgiveness. People separated from God are without hope. Hopeless people become harmful people. Desperation breeds dangerous behavior.

Christians recognize this. They want the world to understand it. That's why the church, passive for so many years, is springing into action. Many are now standing to protest our government's removal of the Ten Commandments.[1] The controversy has ignited a passion and, once again, the church has spun its spotlight towards God's Commandments to champion the cause.

Beyond question, the Christian community at large supports most of the Ten Commandments. Still, some questions need answering. It seems to me there's some double-talk going on.

Countless Christians—engaged in the battle to stop the public stripping of God's Commandments—cling to beliefs that contradict their conduct. Seems they have some explaining to do.

Here's a question I would like to ask of them: W*hy is it important for our government to display the Ten Commandments, if you believe they were nailed to the cross?* Or how about this one: *If the Ten Commandments are so important to society, why do you keep only nine?*

If either of these questions could be addressed to you, let me ask another. Have you ever performed an exhaustive study on the Ten Commandment Law of God? You might be a knowledgeable Bible student, perhaps even a pastor. But have you ever searched the Scriptures on this particular subject for yourself?

I hope my question doesn't appear rude. I don't intend to be offensive. I simply say this because I've met so many Christians who once held to those beliefs until they actually searched the Bible for a definitive answer.

In fact, when I first met Shelley Quinn (the co-author of this book) this is what she told me: "All my life I was taught the Ten Commandments had been nailed to the cross. When I accepted God's call to full-time ministry, the Lord impressed me with this thought, 'Forget what you think you know and come sit at My feet—I will teach you.'

"Still, I admit I went to the Bible to prove that my beliefs were accurate. But God proved me wrong!

"As I searched the Bible for myself, I was astonished at how plain the truth was on this matter. I realized there was only one commandment I wasn't obeying—the Sabbath. After studying God's purposes for the Sabbath, I became a joyful Sabbath celebrator!"

Many Christians have shared a similar sequence of events. An in-depth study of Scripture provided overwhelming evidence to correct their beliefs. These same Christians are today celebrating God's Ten Commandments—all of them!

It's my conviction we must trust that God knew exactly what He was doing when He packaged all Ten Commandments together. Yes, He made them one package! In the New Testament book of James, we are warned that if we break one commandment, we are guilty of breaking them all (Ja 2:10).

And let's not overlook the counsel of Christ. He said if we break one of the least of the commandments—or teach others to do the same—we'll be called the "least" in the kingdom of heaven (Mt 5:19). Should we conveniently sweep His instruction under the rug and forget about it?

Most of today's Christian churches do not keep the Ten Commandments as a combined unit. At best, they adhere to only nine. My question is this: *Do we have the authority to choose which of the Ten Commandments we want to keep?*

Sadly, most Christians ignore the one that God established for our joy at the beginning of time. The forgotten commandment is the very one God calls us to *remember* and keep holy—and "wholly" for our time with Him. I'm speaking of God's seventh-day (Saturday) Sabbath.

This may seem an insignificant matter to you right now, but it looms large on the horizon of the immediate future. Bible writers prophesied a power would establish its own agenda and "think" to change the immutable Law of God (the Ten Commandments). We're living in the fulfillment of that prophecy now.

Still, a time approaches when the issue of Sabbath-keeping will determine the allegiance and eternal security of the people of God. The Bible warns this will develop during the closing trials of earth's history.

For this reason, don't you think it's crucial to examine Scripture and ask the Holy Spirit to unveil God's truths?

Whose agenda controls the Christian majority today? There's no doubt in my mind that the blindly-followed agenda did not originate with God, or with man. The archenemy of Christ propelled this plan into practice.

Satan is not only succeeding in his bid to remove the Ten Commandments from our government institutions, he has already succeeded in removing them from the hearts of most Christians today.

Since the Ten Commandment Law of God is a packaged proposal, and breaking one commandment makes us guilty of breaking all, then we must conclude the Ten Commandments have been *twice removed*—not only from our government, but from most of our churches as well.

Bible prophecy forewarns of this phenomenon. But the warning advances beyond what most people might assume. The Ten Commandment controversy takes central stage before Christ's Second Coming.

Come with me and we will examine Scripture to determine what the Bible has to say about this important issue. What was the "written code" that Christ nailed to the cross? Have we, as some believe, been released from keeping all Ten Commandments because we have found "rest" in Jesus and no longer need a Sabbath rest?

Did God transfer His sanctified Sabbath day from Saturday to Sunday at the resurrection of Christ? Do we know why we go to church on Sunday instead of Saturday? How will these truths safeguard us from deadly deception in the *last days?*

Using the Bible as our guide, we will examine all of this and much more in our search for truth on this crucial topic.

Whose agenda are we following? We will find out as we make our way through this study. In the light of His Word, I believe God will clearly reveal the answer. Then, only one question will remain—

Once the truth is revealed, whose agenda will we choose to follow?

---

[1] I realize the motivation for some who stand in protest of our government's removal of the Ten Commandments is support of freedom to express religious beliefs publicly, rather than the actual application of the Law of God.

On the opposite side of the picket line, some who believe in God's Commandments oppose their display based solely on separation of church and state.

For the record, I fully support separation of church and state. A quick review of world history will remind us that at any time the Church has run the state, or vice-versa, the result has been violent persecution.

Still, I support the right to express personal beliefs in both the private and public sector. And perhaps the public display of God's Commandments, shining His light on wanton behavior, would cause people to acknowledge a higher moral law.

2

To Keep
or
Not to Keep?

*J*esus said, "… I am the way, the truth, and the life. No one comes to the Father except through Me. … The Son of Man has come to seek and to save that which was lost" (Jn 14:6 ; Lk 19:10).

Christ is passionate about saving the perishing. He high-lighted His parables of the lost sheep, the lost coin, and the lost son, with tremendous rejoicing over their recovery. The purpose of His coming was to destroy the devil's work—to seek and to save the lost.

People of the Christian faith understand that to be "separate" from the Lord Jesus is to be "lost." As followers of Christ, we are taught that our privilege (and obligation) is to share the Good News of salvation.

God's kingdom advances as those who have been *saved* by Jesus—the way, the truth, and the life—share their testimony and witness to those who are spiritually *lost*. But how do we recognize who is lost?

When we hear a foul-mouthed person using God's name in vain, we believe they need to hear about the holy and righteous God of love. If we see someone living in adultery or worship-

21

ing "other gods," we understand they are not united with Christ. If we read about a man who just robbed a bank or committed murder, we know he needs to experience the saving power of Jesus.

Whenever a person's actions reflect a glaring disregard for God's Commandments, we recognize they are separated from Jesus. The Bible labels them as lost—*spiritually dead*.

"Now by this we know that we know Him, if we keep His commandments. He who says, 'I know Him,' and does not keep His commandments, is a liar, and the truth is not in him" (1 Jn 2:3-4).

Can anyone know Christ without obeying His commandments? Read that verse again. Then consider how John tells us to identify those who are the children of God: "If you know that He is righteous, you know that everyone who practices righteousness is born of Him" (1 Jn 2:29).

Disobedience to God's commandments is the opposite of practicing righteousness. In fact, did you know that is how the Bible defines sin?

"Whoever commits sin also commits lawlessness, and sin is lawlessness" (1 Jn 3:4). There you have it—the only definition of sin in the Bible. Sin is lawlessness, the breaking of God's Law! Sin separates us from God. Separation from God robs us of eternal life with Him.

"He who sins is of the devil, for the devil has sinned from the beginning ..." (1 Jn 3:8). Satan is the master separator. His objective is to cause separation between God and us through the introduction of sin.

Why do Christians consider actions such as taking God's name in vain, serving other so-called gods, dishonoring parents, murder, adultery, stealing, lying, and coveting as sinful? Because we know these acts break the Law of God.

But there's more to God's Ten Commandment Law, and that presents us with a problem.

To Keep or Not to Keep?

How would you react if I used the fourth commandment to illustrate "lawlessness" that could separate you from a loving Savior? When I suggest that ignoring God's seventh-day (Saturday) Sabbath is the breaking of God's law, many Christians change camps.

The same people who were saying "amen" to the list of sins reviewed above hop to the other side and say, "Wait a minute! The Ten Commandments were nailed to the cross. They're no longer valid."

Seems as though people in this camp choose to believe the only commandment nailed to the cross was God's holy Sabbath—the day God set aside for developing an intimate relationship with Him.

I'm delighted the Bible declares the "handwriting of ordinances" was nailed to the cross. We will discuss this in depth. I hope Scripture will prove to you this verse refers to the Law of Moses.

Among other Bible evidence we examine, we'll see if God's Sabbath was instituted at Creation and if His commandments were known before Mt. Sinai. Did the great forefathers Abraham, Isaac, and Jacob, keep *all* of God's Ten Commandment Law?

But for now, let me toss out a few "teasers" for those who think God's seventh-day (Saturday) Sabbath was canceled at the Cross—

1. "And pray that your flight may not be in winter or on the Sabbath" (Mt 24:20).

    In the context of this Bible passage (Mt 24:15-24), Jesus warned of a time of tribulation that would occur many years *after His death.* If Jesus knew the Sabbath would no longer be in effect after His resurrection, why did He instruct His followers to pray their flight would not be on the Sabbath?

2. "For assuredly, I say to you, till heaven and earth pass away, one jot or one tittle will by no means pass from the law till all is fulfilled" (Mt 5:18).

    We know Christ referred to the Ten Commandment Law here. In the context of this passage, Christ amplified the Commandments—expanding them from the mere "letter" of the law to include the "spirit" of the law. He identified spewing anger and abusive language with the spirit of murder (vs 21-23). He labeled lust as spiritual adultery (vs 27-28).

    Don't you think if Jesus intended to abolish the Sabbath commandment at His resurrection, He would surely have testified that the law of God would be changed *before* heaven and earth passed away?

    The Old Testament prophecies concerning the coming Messiah and the end of the world will not be completely fulfilled until God's people finally put on immortality at the "last trumpet" (See 1 Cor 15:50-58).

3. The Lord says, "For as the new heavens and the new earth which I will make shall remain before Me … it shall come to pass that … from one Sabbath to another, all flesh shall come to worship before Me …" (Is 66:22-23).

    If the Sabbath was removed at His resurrection because we have found rest in Christ, why would God reinstate it in the new heavens and the new earth? For all of eternity, God's redeemed people will gather every seventh-day Sabbath to have a time of special worship and fellowship with our Creator God.

4. "Remember the Sabbath day, to keep it holy." (Ex 20:8) Why is the fourth commandment the only one of the Ten that starts with the word "Remember"?

Do you know what surprises me the most? Many churches agree God's Ten Commandment Law is still in effect today, but they choose to ignore the fourth commandment. In this book, we'll refer to commandment-supportive statements from Catholics, Baptists, Methodists, Lutherans, Episcopalians, and others.

All of these confirm that the seventh-day (Saturday) Sabbath of the fourth commandment was never changed or "done away with" in the New Testament. In fact, they confess Sunday-keeping is the result of the tradition of man, rather than God-inspired instruction from the Holy Bible.

They even go so far as to admit there is not one Scripture in the entire Bible that authorizes the transfer of the Sabbath from Saturday to Sunday. It's clear to all of these Christians that God never ordained the change which man has made to His Law. Yet, they practice man's tradition of Sunday-keeping.

Here's what Spurgeon, the popular nineteenth-century Baptist, said regarding God's Commandments—

"The law of God is a divine law, holy, heavenly, perfect. Those who find fault with the law, or in the least degree depreciate it, do not understand its design, and have no right idea of the law itself. Paul says, 'The law is holy, but I am carnal; sold under sin.' In all we ever say concerning justification by faith, we never intend to lower the opinion which our hearers have of the law, for the law is one of the most sublime of God's works. ...

"There is not a commandment too many; there is not one too few; but it is so *incomparable,* that its *perfection* is a proof of its divinity. No human lawgiver could have given forth such a law as that which we find in the Decalogue [the Ten Commandments]. It is a perfect law; for all human laws that are right are to be found in that brief compendium and epitome of all that is good and excellent toward God; or between man and man" (C. H. Spurgeon, *Sermons,* 2nd series, sermon 18, p. 280).

"The law of the LORD is perfect, converting the soul ..."

(Ps 19:7). Can mere mortal men afford to change, delete, or ignore even *one* of God's perfect set of Ten Commandments? What prompts sincere, God-fearing Christians to ignore the Lord's specific instructions concerning the fourth commandment?

As you read further, you'll discover the Bible declares there would be a conspiracy to destroy God's Commandments, especially the fourth. In our study of Scripture, we'll expose the reason and the power behind it.

The Ten Commandments—*to keep or not to keep?* This is a serious question. It becomes the pivotal issue as we approach the closing crisis of earth's history.

You owe it to yourself to examine this important topic in the light of God's Scriptures to find the answer. It's imperative you know the truth.

In this study, we will closely examine why Satan wants the fourth commandment separated from the Law of God. We will detect his plan to deceive the multitudes of people on Planet Earth into resigning allegiance to him, instead of living in loyalty to our Creator God.

But, you might think, *can the majority of Bible believers be wrong on this issue?* Let me ask you this—weren't the majority of Bible believers walking in error at Christ's first coming?

I don't think we can trust what the "majority" practices. Jesus warned that the masses would follow the broad path that leads to destruction. In contrast, He said the gate that leads to eternal life is narrow—and only a few find it (Mt 7:13-14).

Satan desires to destroy us by causing a separation between our heavenly Father and us. Sin causes separation. As we reviewed, the Bible definition for "sin" is the transgression, or breaking, of God's Ten Commandment Law. You can search the Bible from Genesis to Revelation and you will find no other definition of sin.

Sharing this truth in the past, I have been shocked at the

reaction of some who have said, "Well—that's *your* opinion!" I assure you that it's not just my personal belief.

Listen to what Billy Graham said: "Like Wesley, I find that I must preach the law and judgment before I can preach grace and love. ... The Ten Commandments ... are the moral laws of God for the conduct of people. Some think they have been revoked. That is not true. Christ taught the law. They are still in effect today. God has not changed. People have changed ... .

"Every person who ever lived, with the exception of Jesus Christ, has broken the Ten Commandments. Sin is a transgression of the law. The Bible says all have sinned and come short of the glory of God. The Ten Commandments are a mirror to show us how far short we fall in meeting God's standards. And the mirror of our shortcomings drives us to the Cross, where Christ paid the debt for sin. Forgiveness is found at the Cross, and no other place, according to the Bible ..." (George Burnham and Lee Fisher, *Billy Graham and the New York Crusade*, pp. 108, 109).

Jesus came to save humanity by destroying the works of the devil. "If you abide in My word, you are My disciples indeed. And you shall know the truth, and the truth shall make you free" (Jn 8:31-32). Truth is a Person—and Christ claimed that prerogative, "I am ... the truth" (Jn 14:6). When we walk in the truth of our loving Savior, He will indeed set us free.

I pray, by God's grace, to present the most beautiful Jesus you may have ever seen by presenting the truth of God's Law. What do I mean? As we study further, we will find that the Ten Commandment Law of God is really a transcript, a mirror-image reflection, of God's own character of love.

The little chart that follows will provide a glimpse of how the Ten Commandment Law of God reflects His character. The Holy Spirit inspired men to record the wonders of God's character that He demonstrated to them in His Law.

CHARACTER	TEN COMMANDMENT LAW
God is Perfect	Law is Perfect (Ps 19:7; Ja 1:25)
God is Holy	Law is Holy (Rom 7:12)
God is Spirit	Law is Spiritual (Rom 7:14)
God is Love	Law is Love (1 Tim 1:5; Rom 13:10)
God is Light	Law is Light (Prov 6:23)
God is True	Law is True (Neh 9:13; Ps 119:142, 151)
God is Righteous	Law is Righteous (Rom 8:4)
God is Righteousness	Law is Righteousness (Ps 119:172)
God is Just	Law is Just (Rom 7:12)
God is Pure	Law is Pure (Ps 19:8)
God is Good	Law is Good (Rom 7:12; 1 Tim 1:8)
God is Faithful	Law is Faithful (Ps 119:86)
God is Wisdom	Law is Wisdom (Ps 111:10; Ps 119:98)
God is Great	Law is Great (Hos 8:12)
God is the God of Peace	Love of the Law Brings Great Peace (Ps 119:165)
God is Unchanging	Law is Unchanging (Mt 5:18)

My prayer is that God will lead all into an intimate knowledge of "the way, the truth and the life." I pray the Holy Spirit will destroy the doubts and deceptions the devil has dished out regarding the Law of God.

And I pray Christ will seek and save that which was lost by the majority—the truth of His Ten Commandment Law.

3

Two Laws, Two Covenants—Unraveled

Part 1

"Y our words were found, and I ate them, and Your word was to me the joy and rejoicing of my heart; for I am called by Your name, O LORD God of hosts" (Jer 15:16).

Isn't it exciting when God's truths are revealed to us? When the Holy Spirit illuminates our understanding of Scripture—exposing the essence of God's truth that was veiled before—we have reason to rejoice. God is speaking to us!

Unfortunately, the demands of our fast-paced, high-tech, multi-media world compete with our devotion to Bible study. Compete and—too often—win! The majority of today's time-starved Christians spend little effort in serious Bible study.

Most Christians rely only on what we have been taught by our denomination. We know *what* we believe, but we can't always explain from Scripture *why* we believe it. This leaves us in a precarious spiritual position.

There are so many conflicting convictions within the Christian community. How do we know—with certainty—that what we believe *is* the truth? There's only one way. We must search the Scriptures for ourselves.

Jesus said if we continue in His Word, we will know the truth—and the truth will set us free (Jn 8:31-32).

Perhaps one of the most misunderstood Bible truths today is the difference between the two great divisions of *"the law."* This misunderstanding causes confusion over the contrast between the Old and New Covenants.

In this chapter and the next, we will examine what the Bible reveals on these topics and unravel the truth. This concise overview was written for the time-starved Christian. In just a short while, you will clearly understand how Scripture defines the two great laws of the Bible, and the Old and New Covenants.

"Be diligent to present yourself approved to God, a worker who does not need to be ashamed, rightly dividing the word of truth" (2 Tim 2:15).

Do you want to know for yourself what the Bible really says and means? This study will help to make the truth plain and simple. This will lay a critical foundation for understanding God's Word and His will for you today.

The Two Great Laws of the Bible

Many Christians think the Ten Commandment Law of God was nailed to the cross. They base this belief on Colossians 2: 14, "Blotting out the handwriting of ordinances that was against us, which was contrary to us, and took it out of the way, nailing it to his cross" (KJV).

It's critical to determine the exact nature of this *"handwriting of ordinances"*—this written code with all of its regulations and requirements—that was nailed to the cross. Was it the Ten Commandments of God? Or was it really the Book of the Law, written by Moses?

The Bible speaks of two great "laws"—

1. The Law of God (the "Ten Commandments"), also

known as the Moral Law, the Law of Love, and the Decalogue.

2. The Law of Moses (the "Book of the Law," or "Book of the Covenant"), also known as the Ceremonial Law and the Mosaic Law.

God uniquely calculated the marvelous purposes that He wanted each of these two laws to serve. But, a dim understanding of the differences between the two has led many sincere-hearted Christians into confusion—particularly in interpreting New Testament references to *the law.*

Why is there so much confusion? Bible writers often use the singular word "law" to refer to either the *Law of God* or the *Law of Moses.* If we don't have a clear understanding of their different purposes, it's easy to miss the context of the writings and arrive at misguided conclusions.

For example, Paul wrote: "For as many as are of the works of the law are under the curse. ... No one is justified by the law. ... The law is not of faith. ... Christ has redeemed us from the curse of the law" (Gal 3:10-13).

Yet, he was also inspired to write this: "Do we then make void the law through faith? Certainly not! On the contrary, we establish the law. ... Therefore the law *is* holy, and the commandment holy and just and good." (Rom 3:31, 7:12)

Can you identify which of the two laws Paul was referring to in these passages? By the end of this study, you will know that in Galatians 3:10-13, he referred to the *Law of Moses*—in Romans 3:31 and 7:12, he referred to the Ten Commandment *Law of God,* established in our hearts by faith.

Have you ever felt there was a cloud of confusion that overshadows Paul's writings? That haze will evaporate in a hurry as we examine the differences between these laws.

With increased understanding, you can come to the New Testament and rightly divide the word of truth. When you read the Apostle Paul's writings on "the law," you will be able to search the context and determine whether he was referring to the Law of God, or the Law of Moses.

Paul was the author of the book of Colossians. Under divine inspiration, he wrote that Christ nailed to the cross the "handwriting of ordinances" which stood *against* us. A misguided interpretation has some people claiming Paul taught the Law of God is obsolete.

When you complete this chapter and the next, I hope you see that Paul never intended for the ordinances *against* us to be confused with God's Ten Commandment Law. We will let the Bible prove Paul never dismissed the Ten Commandment Law that God wrote with His own finger on stone tablets.

Bible Scriptures aren't contradictory. Bible writers don't oppose one another. Contradictions stem from pulling Scripture out of context and misapplying it. At first glance, some texts may *appear* to disagree with another. In these cases, it's important to examine the context first, and then research other Bible teachings on the topic.

Sometimes it's necessary to consult the original language in which the texts were written to understand fully the application of the writer's choice of words. Are you like me, considering yourself to do well just to speak English? That's not a problem for Bible students today—even for those of us who are "language challenged." Many study aids are available that can provide us with increased understanding of Greek and Hebrew words.

"All Scripture *is* given by inspiration of God, and *is* profitable for doctrine, for reproof, for correction, for instruction in righteousness, that the man of God may be complete, thoroughly equipped for every good work" (2 Tim 3:16-17).

When Paul wrote these words, he was referring to the Old Testament. Still, his statement is also true of the New Testament. His reference was inspired to be *inclusive*, not *exclusive*.

You can be certain that God never contradicted Himself when He shared His divine thoughts with the many writers of the Bible. Do you see why there can be no disagreement between the writings of the Old and the New Testaments? If we're puzzled by what appears to be contradictory, we must search the Scriptures of both Testaments to overcome our limited understanding.

Some people claim to be "New Testament Christians," implying they consult the New Testament alone for teachings. Unfortunately, someone taught these well-intentioned believers that the New Testament cancelled the teachings of the Old. Paul disagrees. He said God inspired "all Scripture" to equip us for good works.

The Old Testament contains a volume of *equipping Scripture* five to six times larger in content than the New. It's impossible to interpret one without the other—the Old Testament contains the New and the New Testament explains the Old. You will find Jesus Christ in every book of the Bible.

The resurrected Christ told His disciples, "These are the words which I spoke to you while I was still with you, that all things must be fulfilled which were written in the Law of Moses and the Prophets and the Psalms concerning Me" (Lk 24:44).

Jesus also said, "Therefore every scribe instructed concerning the kingdom of heaven is like a householder who brings out of his treasure *things* new and old" (Mt 13:52).

There are spiritual treasures in the Old and New Testaments. The error of tossing out the Old Testament has closed the door to understanding the *eternal* nature of the Ten Commandment Law of God.

Did you know the Old Testament reveals God's Law was in force before He handed it down in stone on Mt. Sinai? We'll look at this in chapter five, where we'll learn God's people violated His Ten Commandments, which obliged God to institute the Law of Moses.

If we throw out the Old Testament, we can't know that Moses wrote the Book of the Law (the "Law of Moses"), or that he recorded approximately 640 separate *ordinances* in his own handwriting. Without this understanding, how could we begin to appreciate that the "handwriting of ordinances" nailed to the cross was the Law of Moses? How could we learn that God's moral law—the Ten Commandments—is eternal and the only definition of sin in the Bible?

"Whoever commits sin also commits lawlessness, and sin is lawlessness" (1 Jn 3:4). Sin is ignoring the Law of God. We recognize murder, theft, lying, adultery, hatred, profanity and all manner of sin exist today.

Isn't it true that our world is in chaos because of sin? In order for us to acknowledge there is sin in the world, there must be a law in force that identifies sin as "sin."

The Old and the New Testaments agree, "The soul who sins shall die. ... For the wages of sin *is* death ..." (Ez 18:20; Rom 6:23). It's impossible for sin to exist *unless* there *is* a law that defines it.

We can apply this principle to the beginning of time, when there were only two created persons on our planet. God instructed Adam and Eve, "You are free to eat from any tree in the garden; but you must not eat from the tree of the knowledge of good and evil ..." (Gen 2:16-17).

God warned they would die if they sinned by ignoring this simple law. Doesn't history record that they ate from the prohibited tree? And what happened? They suffered spiritual death immediately and physical death eventually. That's the wages of sin!

But if God had not laid down the law, they could have savored the succulent fruit without suffering consequences. Without a law to break, they could not have been guilty of "lawlessness." Sin can't exist unless there is a law in place to define it.

34

Let's fast forward to today—is all of humanity guilty of sin? What does the Bible say? "If we say that we have no sin, we deceive ourselves, and the truth is not in us." (1 Jn 1:8). To arrive at a greater understanding of sin, let's examine the two great Bible laws.

Does Scripture prove the Ten Commandment Law of God is *eternal?* In contrast, does Scripture demonstrate the Law of Moses was added as a *temporary* plan to remedy violation of God's Law? Did God ordain the second division of law (Moses' Law) to remain in force *only* until Christ established the New Covenant at the cross? Does the New Covenant contain the Ten Commandments?

The Bible makes it clear and simple to understand—*and there is nothing more important for this generation to grasp!*

The Ten Commandment Law of God

When Moses reviewed the Ten Commandments with the people, he said, "These words the LORD spoke to all your assembly, in the mountain from the midst of the fire, the cloud, and the thick darkness, with a loud voice; and He added no more. And He wrote them on two tablets of stone and gave them to me" (Deut 5:22).

God spoke the Ten Commandments. They were complete. He wrote them on the two tablets. Look at that verse again—take notice that "he added *NO MORE.*" God's law was perfect and He was satisfied to add nothing more to His Ten Commandments.

As the verse we just read pointed out, God first spoke His Commandments to the entire trembling assembly at Mt. Sinai (Ex 20:1-17). But because the people feared the Presence of the Lord, they requested that God speak directly to Moses from that day forth. That's why Moses went alone to Mt. Sinai to receive the engraved stone record of God's Commandments.

Another account of God delivering His commandments to Moses reveals this—

"… He gave Moses two tablets of the Testimony, tablets of stone, written with the finger of God" (Ex 31:18). God engraved—in stone—His Ten Commandment Law *with His own finger*. He didn't leave it up to man to write His "two tablets of the Testimony."

The Bible says God wrote on each side, front and back, of both tablets. We are reassured again that it was God's doing. "Now the tablets *were* the work of God, and the writing *was* the writing of God engraved on the tablets" (Ex 32:15-16). However, who wrote the second set after the first stone tablets were shattered?

You're probably familiar with the part of the story when Moses climbed down the mountain, witnessed the idolatry of the people worshiping the golden calf, and in a fit of righteous indignation slammed the first stone tablets to the ground (Ex 32:19).

But did you know that following this event God still didn't entrust a man to write His Law in a permanent stone record? That's right—not even the second time around (Ex 34:1).

This is how Moses described the second memorial of the Ten Commandments. "At that time the LORD said to me, 'Hew for yourself two tablets of stone like the first, and come up to Me on the mountain and make yourself an ark of wood. And I will write on the tablets the words that were on the first tablets, which you broke; and you shall put them in the ark.' So I made an ark … hewed two tablets of stone … went up the mountain … And He wrote on the tablets according to the first writing, the Ten Commandments …" (Deut 10:1-4).

God wrote the second set with His own finger and instructed Moses to put His two tablets of the Testimony *inside* the Ark. The faithful servant Moses did as God instructed—

"He took the Testimony and put *it* into the ark … and put

the mercy seat on top of the ark" (Ex 40:20). The Ten Commandments were placed *inside* the Ark of the Covenant, in the Most Holy Place of the Tabernacle. Have you ever considered what this illustrated?

The Ark represented God's throne of authority. God instructed Moses to place His Ten Commandment Law in a permanent place, inside the ark (Deut 10:2). From His ark-seat of judgment, God founded His reign on the rule of His Ten Commandments—the transcript of His righteous character.

"The LORD was pleased for His righteousness' sake to make the law great and glorious" (Is 42:21 NASB).

What do we know about God's Law so far? Let's review—

- God's Law was perfect when He spoke it and He added nothing more to His Ten Commandments.
- The Ten Commandments were engraved in stone and called the "two tablets of the Testimony."
- God wrote the Ten Commandments (both sets) with His own finger.
- The Ten Commandments were placed inside the Ark of the Covenant.

The Book of the Law—The Law of Moses

Now, let's briefly review the Law of Moses. I think you will enjoy this, because in just a few paragraphs you will understand the Old Covenant from God's point of view.

The Old Covenant was an expression of God's commitment to rescue the world from sin through Israel. Moses wrote the covenant terms in the *Book of the Covenant,* which the Bible also refers to as the *Book of the Law.*

This is the time-line of the Mt. Sinai events recorded in Exodus: God speaks the Ten Commandments to all the assembly (Ex 20:1-17). The people ask Moses to be their go-between with God (Ex 20:18-19). God speaks to Moses the words of the special covenant with Israel (Ex 20:22-23:33). Moses recites the covenant and its judgments to the people (Ex 24:3). Moses writes the Book of the Covenant, builds an altar, and confirms the covenant with sacrificial blood (Ex 24:4-8). Moses goes up the mountain for forty days and nights (Ex 24:12-18). God writes the Ten Commandments in stone and gives them to Moses (Ex 31:18). Moses breaks the two tablets (Ex 32:19). God writes the second set of tablets with His own finger and gives them to Moses (Ex 34:1).

After God spoke His Ten Commandment Law to the assembly, Moses alone drew near to God. The Lord gave him special civil laws and ceremonial ordinances for Israel to follow. When Moses returned from his meeting, he recited these special contract terms to the people and they agreed to do all that the Lord had spoken.

It's interesting to note the contrast here. It was God Who spoke the Ten Commandments to all the people before etching them in stone. But when the conditions of the special covenant contract between God and Israel were announced to the nation, Moses stood in as the mediator between them.

Exodus, chapter twenty-four, tells how Moses then wrote all the words of the Lord in the "Book of the Covenant" and built an altar. Before He confirmed the covenant with sacrificial blood, he read all the words he had written in the *Book of the Covenant* to the people.

Again, they accepted the terms and declared their covenant obedience. So Moses took the blood and sprinkled both the book itself and all the people (Heb 9:19; Ex 24:8) and said, "This is the blood of the covenant which the LORD has made with you according to all these words" (Ex 24:7-8).

"So it was, when Moses had completed writing the words of this law in a book, when they were finished, that Moses commanded the Levites, who bore the ark of the covenant of the LORD, saying: 'Take this Book of the Law, and put it beside the ark of the covenant of the LORD your God, that it may be there as a witness against you'" (Deut 31:24-26).

Moses wrote these special covenant ordinances—in his own handwriting—in the Book of the Law *(Book of the Covenant)*. An animal sacrifice provided the "blood of the covenant" God made with Israel. This Book of the Law (the handwriting of ordinances) was positioned in a *temporary* place, *beside* the ark, and it stood there as a *witness against the people.*

Why did the Law of Moses stand as a witness against this rebellious people? The Bible reveals this sobering answer, as a warning to those who turned away from God to serve other *gods*—

"… Every curse that is written in this book would settle on him, and the LORD would blot out his name from under heaven … according to all the curses of the covenant that are written in this Book of the Law," (Deut 29:20-21). In addition to the blessings God promised Israel for their faithfulness (Ex 34:10, Deut 28:1-14), the *Book of the Law* contained curses against those who did not meet all of its requirements.

An all-loving God knows that sin causes pain and destruction. The Lord meant for the curses of the *Book of the Law* to serve as a deterrent to sin. When He came as the Redeemer of Israel, He gave them commandments for their benefit—

"… I am the LORD your God, Who teaches you to profit, Who leads you by the way you should go. Oh, that you had heeded My commandments! Then your peace would have been like a river, and your righteousness like the waves of the sea" (Is 48:17-18).

God's discipline has always flowed from a heart of love, to protect His children from sin's fatal force. God takes no pleasure in the death of the wicked (Ez 33:11).

"Have you not brought this on yourself, in that you have forsaken the LORD your God when He led you in the way? Your own wickedness will correct you, and your backslidings will rebuke you ..." (Jer 2:17, 19).

When sinners die, it is the direct consequence of their own choices. The patience and goodness of God to the people under the Old Covenant is very apparent in Scripture. The special covenant He made with Israel was to teach crucial lessons to save the nation.

Unfortunately, the Jewish nation began to apply the *Book of the Law* as a means by which to obtain righteousness—twisting God's purpose to their own destruction. Centuries later, Paul commented on this by saying if righteousness could have been obtained through the Law of Moses, then Christ died in vain (Gal 2:21).

The only kind of righteousness that has ever existed from God's viewpoint is *righteousness by faith.* Yes, even under the Old Covenant, the true followers of God knew they could not *earn* righteousness. Jeremiah declared God's name to be this: "... THE LORD OUR RIGHTEOUSNESS" (Jer 23:6).

And Hosea cried out, "Sow for yourselves righteousness; reap in mercy; break up your fallow ground, for it is time to seek the LORD, till He comes and rains righteousness on you" (Hos 10:12).

Isaiah knew the best that man could offer God paled in comparison to God's holiness: "For we have all become like one who is unclean ... and all our righteousness (our best deeds of rightness and justice) is like filthy rags" (Is 64:6 AMP).

He also declared this: "I will greatly rejoice in the LORD, My soul shall be joyful in my God; for He has clothed me with the garments of salvation, He has covered me with the robe of righteousness ..." (Is 61:10).

The Law of Moses described ceremonies and practices given to Israel that pointed forward to Jesus as the true Lamb of God. Because of this, it sometimes was referred to as the *Ceremonial Law,* and had a limited time of effectiveness attached to it. The New Testament writer of Hebrews points out its purpose—

"It *was* symbolic for the present time in which both gifts and sacrifices are offered which cannot make him who performed the service perfect in regard to the conscience—concerned *only* with foods and drinks, various washings, and fleshly ordinances imposed until the time of reformation" (Heb 9:9-10).

Simply put, the Law of Moses was merely a lesson book to prepare God's people for the time when Christ would come to bring reformation.

The Law of Moses was a special contract God made with the Israelites. Paul clearly defined the *Old Covenant* as Moses' writings (*the Book of the Law*)—

"… For until this very day at the reading of the old covenant [literal Greek translation] the same veil remains unlifted, because it is removed in Christ. But to this day whenever Moses is read, a veil lies over their heart; but whenever a person turns to the Lord, the veil is taken away." (2 Cor 3:14-16 NASB).

The *Book of the Covenant* and the *Book of the Law* are one and the same. Bible writers used the terms interchangeably. In 2 Kings 22:8, the high priest found the "Book of the Law in the house of the Lord." When King Josiah assembled the nation and read to them all the words of the Book, he referred to it as the *Book of the Covenant*—

"And he read in their hearing all the words of the Book of the Covenant which had been found in the house of the LORD. … Then the king commanded all the people, saying, 'Keep the Passover to the LORD your God, as *it is* written in this Book of the Covenant'" (2 Kings 23:2, 21). We find the exact language repeated in another account of this same event recorded in 2 Chronicles 34:14-15 and verse 30.

The Old Covenant was contained in the writings of

41

Moses—the *Book of the Law*—not the Ten Commandment Law of God alone. There is no doubt, however, that the Ten Commandments were the central part of the Old Covenant. The Bible says Moses wrote *all* the words spoken by the Lord in his book. And Moses confirmed this when he said—

"So He declared to you His covenant which He commanded you to perform, the Ten Commandments; and He wrote them on two tablets of stone. And the LORD commanded me at that time to teach you statutes and judgments, that you might observe them in the land which you cross over to possess" (Deut 4:13-14). And Moses called the tablets of stone the "tablets of the covenant" (Deut 9:11). God's Ten Commandments were the heart of the covenant.

Let's sum up what we already know about the Law of Moses:

- The Law of Moses was written in Moses' own handwriting.
- The Mosaic Law contained civil laws and ceremonial ordinances.
- It was written on a parchment scroll and called the "Book of the Law" or "Book of the Covenant."
- It contained curses against those who did not obey the works of the Law of Moses.
- The Book of the Law was placed on the *side* of the ark—as a witness against Israel.
- The Law of Moses was symbolic and temporary.
- The Law of Moses was the Old Covenant contract made with Israel.
- The Book of the Law embraced the Ten Commandments as the central part of the covenant.

Now that we are armed with accurate information on the Ten Commandment *Law of God* and the *Law of Moses*, let's see how this knowledge can help us understand New Testament references to "the law."

As we continue part two of this study in the next chapter, the Holy Spirit will illuminate our understanding of the New Covenant. And Scripture will prove—beyond any doubt—exactly what Christ nailed to the cross!

God's words were found—and you ate them. I hope, as for me, they will be the rejoicing of your heart. God is speaking to us through His Word. We have reason to rejoice!

4

Two Laws, Two Covenants—Unraveled

Part 2

Many people are puzzled by New Testament references to "the law." Some feel that Paul speaks from both sides of his mouth. Trying to understand his writings on the law simply stumps them, so they seize hold of the Scriptures that support their way of thinking—ignoring the rest.

But we no longer have to be counted in that number. Now that we know the distinct differences of the Ten Commandment *Law of God* and the *Law of Moses,* we have the advantage of understanding New Testament references to *the law* in the context of the passage.

In the previous chapter, our Bible review proved that the *Old Covenant* was the *Law of Moses*—recorded in the *Book of the Covenant (Book of the Law)*

The Old Testament proved to us beyond doubt that the Ten Commandments alone were *not* the Old Covenant. The significance of the great Ten was that they were the *heart* of the special covenant God made with Israel.

Our review of Old Testament Scriptures revealed that *righteousness by faith* was as much a part of the Old Covenant as it is with the New. Still, God commanded obedience to His right way of doing all things, to shield His children from the ravages of sin.

We also saw that God's Ten Commandment Law was perfect—and He added nothing more. In His great love, God gave His commandments for the benefit of humanity's peace—to lead us in His path of life (Is 48:17-18).

If salvation has always been by grace, through faith, then we must reexamine the definition of the New Covenant. Has man's definition fallen short of God's glorious intent?

And what about the Ten Commandments of God? We saw that they were positioned in a place of permanence—inside His ark-throne. Was the *Law of God* nailed to the cross, or is it a part of the New Covenant? What is the *law of liberty?*

Let's see what the Bible says on these matters!

The New Covenant and the Law

The Ceremonial Law of Moses defined the earthly temple services and all the special *annual* sabbaths. Everything contained within the Ceremonial Law was a shadow that pointed to Jesus as the substance—

"For the law, having a shadow of the good things to come, *and* not the very image of the things, can never with these same sacrifices, which they offer continually year by year, make those who approach perfect" (Heb 10:1).

The Law of Moses prescribed sacrifices, festivals, and ceremonial ordinances that were symbolic of Jesus. Paul emphatically states that the law of ceremonies ended when it was nailed to the cross—

"And you, being dead in your sins and the uncircumcision of your flesh, hath he quickened together with him, having forgiven you all trespasses; Blotting out the handwriting of ordinances that was against us, which was contrary to us, and took it out of the way, nailing it to his cross" (Col 2:13-14 KJV).

Be sure to note here that the Bible says the *handwriting of ordinances* (the Law of Moses) was nailed to the cross—not the Ten Commandment Law of God!

In this same passage of Scripture, Paul continued to write, "So let no one judge you in food or in drink, or regarding a festival or a new moon or sabbaths, which are a shadow of things to come, but the substance is of Christ" (Col 2:16-17).

All of the ceremonial ordinances, including the special annual sabbaths (not to be confused with the weekly, seventh-day Sabbath) were merely a shadowy symbol of the ministry of Christ.

Christ made it clear that the purpose of the Law of Moses was to prepare the people for His arrival when He said—

"… These *are* the words which I spoke to you while I was still with you, that all things must be fulfilled which were written in the Law of Moses and *the* Prophets and *the* Psalms concerning Me" (Lk 24:44).

Paul wrote that Christ was the end—the *aim* or the *goal*—of the Law. "For Christ *is* the end of the law for righteousness to everyone who believes. For Moses writes about the righteousness which is of the law, 'The man who does those things shall live by them'" (Rom 10:4-5).

We must carefully consider the context of Paul's writings. Which law was he referring to?

In the previously quoted Scriptures, notice that Paul clarifies he is speaking of the Law of Moses when he speaks of the *writing of Moses* and quotes what the Lord had spoken to Moses regarding the *Book of the Law:* "You shall therefore keep My statutes and My judgments, which if a man does, he shall live by them …" (Lev 18:5).

Can you clearly see what Paul was saying in Romans 10:4-5? Christ was the end—the *aim* or the goal—of the Law of Moses, the Old Covenant that expressed God's commitment to rescue the world from sin.

Christ is our *New Covenant* with God! In a Messianic prophecy about Christ, God said—

"I, the LORD, have called You in righteousness, and will hold Your hand; I will keep You and give You as a covenant to the people, as a light to the Gentiles, to open blind eyes, to bring out prisoners from the prison, those who sit in darkness from the prison house" (Is 42:6-7).

There's no doubt the New Covenant we celebrate in Jesus contains the Ten Commandments. Listen to what the Lord says—

"… Behold, the days are coming, says the LORD, when I will make a new covenant. … This *is* the covenant … I will put My laws in their mind and write them on their hearts; and I will be their God, and they shall be My people" (Heb 8:8,10 – *see also* Jer 31:31-33).

The Ten Commandment Law of God is the heart of the New Covenant, just as it was in the Old.

Paul plainly taught the Law of God was part of the New Covenant. Notice how he describes the nature of both the Law of Moses (which contained circumcision ordinances) and the Ten Commandment Law of God in this side-by-side comparison—

"Circumcision is nothing and uncircumcision is nothing, but keeping the commandments of God *is what matters*" (1 Cor 7:19).

Let's highlight some points about the New Covenant—

- Christ is our New Covenant (Is 42:6-7). Just as the Old Covenant expressed God's commitment to rescue the world from sin through ceremonies and symbols in the days of Israel, so the New Covenant expresses God's same commitment through Christ—the fulfillment of those symbols.
- Christ humbled Himself and came to earth in the very likeness of humanity (Phil 2:5-8). God sent His Son

in the likeness of sinful flesh to be a sin offering (Rom 8:3). God made Him who knew no sin to be born with our sinful nature (2 Cor 5:21).

Christ was made like us in every way—He shared in our humanity so that He could destroy the works of the devil (Heb 2:14, 17). He suffered when He was tempted so that He could help us when we are being tempted (Heb 2:18).

- In spite of His human nature, Christ was sinless—that's why His life can take away our sins (1 Jn 3:5). He was the perfect sacrifice, who died for ungodly sinners to demonstrate God's love for us (Rom 5:6, 8). Our old sin nature was crucified with Him—nailed to the cross—so that we don't have to be slaves to sin any longer (Rom 6:6).

- Humanity is born with the sinful nature of Adam (after his fall), but Jesus Christ offers us a new nature (1 Cor 15:45). With His empowering life in us, born-again disciples can follow in His righteous footsteps as our pathway (Ps 85:13; 1 Jn 2:6). We can walk in loving obedience to the Father's will.

- The Ten Commandments are the heart of the New Covenant (Heb 8:8, 10; Jer 31:31-33). They are really ten wonderful promises of how the life of Christ in us will empower us to demonstrate our love for God and for humanity. God will work in us to cause us to desire His ways and to act according to His good purposes (Phil 2:13).

Can you see that the difference between the time of Moses (Old Covenant) and the time of Christ (New Covenant) is not the abolishing of the Ten Commandments? The real difference is the path to salvation.

The old ceremonial Law of Moses established a temporary

set of symbolic acts that represented the ministry of the coming Messiah, Jesus Christ. Under the ceremonial law, a sinner sacrificed an innocent lamb to cover their sin.

Sin was symbolically transferred to the blameless sacrifice, pointing to Christ becoming our substitute to pay the death penalty our sins required.

"… Behold! The Lamb of God who takes away the sin of the world!" (Jn 1:29). Christ was the spotless Lamb of God. He became the sacrifice for you and me. At the cruel cross of Calvary, God transferred the penalty of death we deserve to His precious Son.

The power of Christ's shed blood is sufficient to cover all our confessed sins. Unlike the priests of the Old Covenant, Christ does not need to make repeated sacrifices. The Bible says He sacrificed "once for all" when He offered up Himself (Heb 7:27).

"And Jesus cried out again with a loud voice, and yielded up His spirit. Then, behold, the veil of the temple was torn in two from top to bottom; and the earth quaked, and the rocks were split" (Mt 27:50-51).

At the crucifixion, God ended the earthly temple services prescribed in the Law of Moses. On that day, when God ripped the veil that covered the entrance to the Most Holy Place, He demonstrated that Christ's sacrifice had given us direct access— through His Son—to His throne of grace.

Before Christ's death on Calvary, only the High Priest had access to the Most Holy Place, and he could enter only once a year. But when the veil was torn, God demonstrated that the symbolic ceremonies had met the Substance—Jesus Christ, the new and living way to the Father.

The Old Covenant was the "Book of the Law" and contained the Ten Commandments. The New Covenant is found in Jesus Christ and still contains the Ten Commandments. With this greater understanding, let's tackle a passage that many interpret to mean God's Commandments were done away with.

It's a writing of Paul, found in Galatians 3:10-14. I'll break it into bite size pieces as we go through it—

- "For as many as are of the works of the law are under the curse; for it is written, 'Cursed *is* everyone who does not continue in all things which are written in the book of the law, to do them.'" *Here, in the context of Gal 3:10, Paul clearly states he is writing about the Book of the Law (the Law of Moses). And he quotes from the Book of the Law, "Cursed is he who does not confirm the words of this law by doing them" (Deut 27:26 NASB).*

- "But that no one is justified by the law in the sight of God *is* evident, for 'the just shall live by faith.'" *Paul continues, in Gal 3:11, to write with the same reference to the Book of the Law. Some misguided souls use this Scripture to try to abolish the Ten Commandments, but we know Paul is referring to the Law of Moses.*

- *Writing about the Law of Moses, He goes on to say in verses 12-14,* "Yet the law is not of faith, but 'the man who does them shall live by them.' Christ has redeemed us from the curse of the law, having become a curse for us (for it is written, 'Cursed *is* everyone who hangs on a tree'), that the blessing of Abraham might come upon the Gentiles in Christ Jesus, that we might receive the promise of the Spirit through faith."

As we've already studied, the curses of the law were written in the Book of the Law—Moses' book. Christ redeemed us from the curse of the Law of Moses.

Do you see how easy it is to understand Paul's writings once you understand the difference between the Law of Moses and the Ten Commandment Law of God?

With a little history on the nature and purpose of the two laws, and by examining the context of the passage, we can distinguish which law Paul was referring to and the exact intent of his writing. We can rightly divide and interpret Scripture.

Within the same chapter and context, Paul explains that God's plan of salvation has always been by grace, through faith. Then he explains why the Law of Moses was instituted in the first place—

"And this I say, *that* the law, which was four hundred and thirty years later, cannot annul the covenant that was confirmed before by God in Christ, that it should make the promise of no effect. For if the inheritance *is* of the law, *it is* no longer of promise; but God gave *it* to Abraham by promise. What purpose then *does* the law *serve*? It was added because of transgressions, till the Seed should come to whom the promise was made; *and it was* appointed through angels by the hand of a mediator" (Gal 3:17-19).

Since we just reviewed Galatians 3:10-14, you can be sure Paul's reference in Galatians 3:17-19 is to the very same Book of the Law.

The Law of Moses was a temporary law, put into effect through angels by Moses, acting as a mediator between God and Israel. There was no mediator when God spoke His Ten Commandments to the entire assembly.

The Law of Moses did not set aside the promise to Abraham of salvation by faith. The Book of the Law was *added* because of *transgressions (sin)*. As we have repeatedly discussed, it's not possible for transgression (sin) to exist unless there is a law in place.

Since God's Ten Commandments were in place before the Law of Moses, we can conclude that Moses' Law was added because God's Moral Law had been violated.

All of the ceremonial laws contained in the Book of Moses

pointed to Jesus. It was only temporary—a law to serve until Jesus (the Seed of God) came to bring a time of reformation (Heb 9:10).

"The law of the LORD *is* perfect, converting the soul …" (Ps 19:7). It is God's Ten Commandment Law that is perfect! The handwriting of ordinances in Moses' Law could not "convert the soul." God's law is perfect because it reflects His perfect nature of love.

The Law of Love and Liberty

The Ten Commandments are the Law of Love—a transcript of God's character!

"He who does not love does not know God, for God is love" (1 Jn 4:8).

The Ten Commandments express God's perfect will of love for His people. Christ's character of love is revealed in the Law of God. Our Lord said all of His Ten Commandments are sustained by love—

"… You shall love the LORD your God with all your heart, with all your soul, and with all your mind. … You shall love your neighbor as yourself. On these two commandments hang all the Law and the Prophets" (Mt 22:37-40).

The first four Commandments (Ex 20:2-11) define how we can develop an intimate love relationship with God—loving the Lord with all of our heart, soul, mind and strength. The final six Commandments (Ex 20:12-17) define how we can love our neighbor as we love ourselves.

Jesus said, "If you love Me, keep My commandments. If you keep My commandments, you will abide in My love, just as I have kept My Father's commandments and abide in His love" (Jn 14:15, 15:10).

Jesus obeyed the Father's commandments. He asks us to demonstrate our love for Him by doing the same.

Paul wrote that love is the fulfillment of the Ten Commandment Law of God (Rom 13:10). In the Greek that means love fills God's Commandments to the fullest. How can we fulfill His Law of Love? It's impossible if we depend on human nature.

The action required of us is to open our hearts and allow God to pour out His love into us by the power of His Holy Spirit (Rom 5:5). God's perfect law is filled to its fullest only by His love flowing through us.

"Here is the patience of the saints; here *are* those who keep the commandments of God and the faith of Jesus" (Rev 14:12).

Revelation, the last book of the Bible, identifies the saints of God as those who are *keeping the commandments of God* and have the faith of Jesus. Revelation also points out Satan's fury against the church who keeps God's commandments—

"And the dragon [symbolic for Satan] was enraged with the woman [symbolic for the church], and he went to make war with the rest of her offspring, who keep the commandments of God and have the testimony of Jesus Christ" (Rev 12:17).

What commandments are these true, end-time Christians keeping? We know theses references are not to the Law of Moses. If God abolished His Ten Commandments, why would the Bible instruct us to "keep the commandments of God"?

The Apostle James clearly defines God's standard of judgment as His Ten Commandment Law—

"If you really fulfill *the* royal law according to the Scripture, 'You shall love your neighbor as yourself,' you do well; but if you show partiality, you commit sin, and are convicted by the law as transgressors. For whoever shall keep the whole law, and yet stumble in one *point*, he is guilty of all. For He who said, 'Do not commit adultery,' also said, 'Do not murder.' Now if you do not commit adultery, but you do murder, you have become a transgressor of the law. So speak and so do as those who will be judged by the law of liberty" (Ja 2:8-12)

The "law of liberty" is this—Christ sets us free from sin and empowers us to walk in obedience to God. He does for us what we cannot do for ourselves, causing us to be all that He has called us to be!

God's Ten Commandments are really ten wonderful promises of what He will do in our lives. Christ came to destroy the works of the devil. He sends His Holy Spirit to give us power over sin.

Since we live in a world of sin, there has to be a law that defines sin. That law is God's Ten Commandments.

James' counsel in the New Testament agrees with the wise counsel Solomon gave in the Old Testament. Their agreement testifies that God's purpose for His Ten Commandment Law is as constant as God Himself—

"Let us hear the conclusion of the whole matter: Fear God and keep His commandments, for this is man's all. For God will bring every work into judgment, including every secret thing, whether good or evil" (Eccl 12:13-14).

God cannot lie or contradict Himself. Sinners today still deserve the wages they have earned. "For the wages of sin *is* death, but the gift of God *is* eternal life in Christ Jesus our Lord" (Rom 6:23).

The privilege we now enjoy is that when we recognize we have sinned, we can go directly to Jesus and ask Him for forgiveness. Christ understands! He lived in this sin-sick world. He understands our struggle with every temptation.

As the one true High Priest, He now intercedes with His Father on our behalf, and He is able to save us completely (Heb 7:25). Instead of eternal death, we receive the gift of eternal life, when we submit to God's will and commit our lives to Him—walking in obedience to His Commandments.

"And having been perfected, He became the author of eternal salvation to all who obey Him" (Heb 5:9).

Christ walked in perfect obedience to the Father—not to

become God's Son, but because He *was* the holy Son of God. He expects us to obey, because He empowers us to obey.

True Christians don't keep God's Commandments *in order* to be saved. We know salvation is a gift—by grace, through faith. True Christians keep God's commandments *because* we are saved, and love for the Lord motivates us to please Him by walking in obedience.

Obedience is the key factor here. One of the lies Satan has been spreading for hundreds of years is that God's Ten Commandments were nailed to the cross. The great deceiver has caused many to believe Christ sacrificed His life so that we would no longer have to walk in obedience to God's perfect Ten Commandment Law.

Christ disagrees! Speaking of the Ten Commandment Law of God, He said—

"Do not think that I came to destroy the Law or the Prophets. I did not come to destroy but to fulfill. For assuredly, I say to you, till heaven and earth pass away, one jot or one tittle will by no means pass from the law till all is fulfilled. Whoever therefore breaks one of the least of these commandments, and teaches men so, shall be called least in the kingdom of heaven; but whoever does and teaches them, he shall be called great in the kingdom of heaven" (Matthew 5:17-19).

Christ came to "fulfill" the Law. In the Greek, the word used here means to *fill it full*—to reveal God's fullest intentions. Christ also declared the Ten Commandment Law of God would endure "till heaven and earth pass away."

Since God revealed His perfect will in His Commandments, do humans have any right to divide it or delete any portion of it? Not even the smallest stroke of writing will be deleted until all is fulfilled at His second coming!

What was nailed to the cross? When Jesus Christ offered Himself as God's perfect sacrifice, He was "blotting out the handwriting of ordinances that was against us, which was contrary to us, and took it out of the way, nailing it to his cross" (Col 2:14 KJV).

Christ nailed the Old Covenant—the ordinances of the Law of Moses—to the cross!

Christ *is* our New Covenant with God! As we partake of His divine nature, we are empowered to walk in His footsteps of obedience to God.

The Ten Commandment *Law of God*—written in our hearts and minds—is the heart of the New Covenant, just as it was with the Old.

The *law of liberty* is this—by the life of Christ working in us and through us, we are empowered to walk in obedience to God's commandments.

Now that we have unraveled the truth about the two great *laws* of the Bible and the Old and New Covenants, we have every reason in the world to rejoice. We can count on our Savior to destroy the devious works of the devil in our lives.

Christ will do for us what we cannot do for ourselves— *causing* us to be all that He has *called* us to be. Hallelujah!

For your easy reference,
a chart is included on the next page
to identify some of the differences between
the Ten Commandment Law of God and the Law of Moses.

The Ten Commandment Law of God	The Law of Moses
Called "The law of the Lord" *Isaiah 5:24*	Called "The law of Moses" *Luke 2:22* *1 Corinthians 9:9*
Written by God on Stone *Exodus 31:18, 32:16*	Written by Moses in a Book *Deuteronomy 31:24* *2 Chronicles 35:12*
Placed inside the Ark *Exodus 40:20*	Placed by the side of the Ark *Deuteronomy 31:26*
God's law points out sin *Romans 7:7, 3:20*	Moses' law added because of sin *Galatians 3:19*
God's law is not grievous *1 John 5:3*	Moses' law was contrary to us *Colossians 2:14*
God's law is called "The Royal Law" *James 2:8*	Moses' law was called "Law contained in the ordinances" *Ephesians 2:15*
God's law judges all men *James 2:10-12*	Moses' law judges no man *Colossians 2:14-16*
God's law is Spiritual *Romans 7:14*	Moses' law was Carnal *Hebrews 7:16*
God's law brings blessings and peace *Proverbs 29:18* *Psalms 119:165*	Moses' law contained curses *Deuteronomy 29:20-21* *Galations 3:10*
God's law is PERFECT *Psalms 19:7*	Moses' law made nothing perfect *Hebrews 7:19*
God's law is ETERNAL *Matthew 5:17-19*	Moses' law was temporary *Colossians 2:14* *Hebrews 8:13*

5

Before Mt. Sinai—
After the Resurrection

hen Moses climbed Mt. Sinai to receive the written record of God's Moral Law, he witnessed the
finger of God carving His perfect set of commandments on the stone "tablets of the Testimony."

Many Christians think this event was the first introduction
of God's commandments to humanity. They mistakenly believe
that Abraham (who lived four centuries before Moses) served
only as the example of salvation by faith, rather than obedience
to God.

It's true that God made an everlasting covenant with the
patriarch Abraham—a covenant of grace—*righteousness by
faith* and not by works (Rom 4:3-8). In vision, Abraham saw
Christ's day and rejoiced (Jn 8:56). He recognized the eternal
covenant would find fulfillment in the ministry of Jesus Christ,
and placed His faith in the Calvary Plan of God.

God *credited* Abraham's faith to his account as righteousness. What does it mean to be made righteous? To be righteous
represents a condition of "right standing" with God.

Still, was God's promise of grace conditional upon obedience? Listen to God's words when He confirmed the oath of the
covenant with Abraham's son, Isaac: "… In your seed all the

nations of the earth shall be blessed; because Abraham obeyed My voice and kept My charge, My commandments, My statutes, and My laws" (Gen 26:4-5).

Does righteousness by faith require a work? The Apostle Peter said, "... God shows no partiality. But in every nation whoever fears Him and works righteousness is accepted by Him" (Acts 10:34-35).

And John wrote, "Let no one deceive you. He who practices righteousness is righteous, just as He is righteous" (1 Jn 3:7). Righteousness defined is to practice God's *right way* of doing all things.

The Bible clearly records that Abraham obeyed God's commandments and laws. Blessings came as the result of obedience. God confirmed the covenant with Abraham's descendents because the patriarch put the righteousness he received from God into practice.

Abraham blazed the trail to blessings for all of his offspring—obedience to God's Commandments! "Therefore know that the LORD your God ... keeps covenant and mercy for a thousand generations with those who love Him and keep His commandments" (Deut 7:9; *see also* Dan 9:4; Neh 1:5).

What laws of God did Abraham obey centuries before Moses? Did man understand the Moral Law before the time of Moses? In order for us to answer these questions, we must review the history of humanity recorded prior to God speaking His commandments to the desert exiles (Exodus 20).

Remember, if there is no commandment in place, there is no sin. With that in mind, let's look at each of the Ten Commandments and see if the patriarchs preceding Moses were aware of God's laws—

1. **The First Commandment is about *loyalty*—*Ex 20:2-3.***
    The Creator of the universe declares He is our God and our Deliverer. He asks us to demonstrate our love for

Him by having no other gods. Jacob (who lived long before Moses) proved he understood this law. He told the people to put away their *foreign gods,* and purify and cleanse themselves from this sin (Gen 35:2-4).

2. **The Second Commandment is about** *worship—Ex 20:4-6.* God prohibits the worship of images, of bowing before a carved statue. The previous account of the "foreign gods" begins in Genesis 31:19-34. Rachel, Jacob's wife, stole the graven images from the home of her idolatrous father. Genesis 35:2 gives evidence the patriarchs knew idol worship was sinful and made a person unclean in the eyes of the Lord.

3. **The Third Commandment is about** *reverence—Ex 20:7.* God instructs us to respect His holy name and not to use His name in vain. In Hebrew *vain* is "shaw" and has a broad meaning—iniquity, falsehood, vanity, emptiness. Simply summed up, *shaw* means showing disrespect.

    There are many instances recorded before Mt. Sinai of the sin of disrespecting the name of the Lord. When Moses relayed God's instruction to release the people of Israel from slavery, Pharaoh scoffed at the authority of God's name (see Exodus 5). The Lord eventually destroyed him because of the hardness of his heart.

4. **The Fourth Commandment is about** *sanctification and relationship—Ex 20:8-11.* God instructs His people to "remember" the Sabbath and keep it set apart for holy purposes to draw nearer to Him. God initiated the Sabbath rest at Creation, blessing and sanctifying the seventh day (Gen 2:1-3). It's clear He expected continued observance.

    Well *before* the Israelites arrived at Mt. Sinai, the Lord ordered preparation for the Sabbath. The people were to gather a double portion of manna on the sixth day, so they could rest on the holy seventh day (Exodus 16:22-26). Some did not heed the instructions and God was displeased—

"Now it happened that some of the people went out on the seventh day to gather, but they found none. And the LORD said to Moses, 'How long do you refuse to keep My commandments and My laws? See! For the LORD has given you the Sabbath; therefore He gives you on the sixth day bread for two days ...'" (Ex 16: 27-29).

5. **The Fifth Commandment is about** *respect for parental authority—Ex 20:12.* God instructs us to show love for our parents by honoring them. Genesis 37: 28-35 and 50:15-17 demonstrates this commandment was also known before Mt. Sinai. These two Bible passages give the account of Joseph and his brothers. It brings to light the sin of disrespecting our parents through dishonesty.

In the first account, the brothers lied to their father about the death of Joseph. In the later account, the brothers ask forgiveness for their trespasses against their father. They knew they had violated the Fifth Commandment. Also, consider the record of Ham dishonoring Noah by exposing the nakedness of his sleeping father. Ham suffered under a lifelong curse for his sin (Gen 9:22-27).

6. **The Sixth Commandment is about** *respect for human life—Ex 20:13.* God instructs us to demonstrate love, not hatred, toward others by not committing murder. The Bible records Cain's guilt of murdering his brother, Abel. God punished Cain for breaking this commandment. This law was obviously in force (Gen 4:8-13).

7. **The Seventh Commandment is about** *purity in relationships—Ex 20:14.* God asks us to demonstrate our love by not committing adultery. Long before Moses' birth, the Bible identifies adultery as sinful in the accounts of Pharaoh taking Abraham's wife into his house (Gen 12:10-20), and Sodom and Gomorrah (Gen 18:20-21).

   The best example to prove God's commandment on adultery was known before Mt. Sinai is the account of Joseph, who refused to have an affair with Potipher's wife saying, in Genesis 39:9, "You *are* his wife. How then can I do this great wickedness, and sin against God?"

8. **The Eighth Commandment is about** *honesty—Ex 20:15.* God instructs us not to steal. The Bible history of Joseph's reunion with his shifty brothers, records that Joseph devised the ultimate test before he revealed his identity to them. He planted a cup in the sack of his youngest brother, Benjamin, to make it appear as if it had been stolen.

   Joseph wanted to create a valid reason to keep his beloved brother with him as the others departed. His test was to see what kind of men the other brothers had become. Their horrified response showed they associated stealing with sin—*in their mind* deserving of death. They knew the commandment of God (Gen 44:4, 6-10).

9. **The Ninth Commandment is about** *truthfulness— Ex 20:16.* The Lord instructs us not to lie or deceive others. Christ proclaimed Satan as the "father of lies" (Jn 8:44). The first recorded lie on planet Earth is recorded in Genesis 3:4, when Satan contradicted God's word and told Eve, "You will not surely die." The story of Jacob and Esau, told partially in Genesis

27, demonstrates that lying and deceit was known to be evil.

10. **The Tenth Commandment is about *contentment*— *Ex 20:17*.** God instructs us not to covet—because He knows it can entrap us in even greater sin. There are many examples of this in early history, but I think one of the more striking accounts is the consequences Eve suffered. She coveted the forbidden fruit and fell into greater sin. Her coveting contributed to her expulsion from the Garden of Eden! And later, her son Cain copied her sin.

   When Cain brought an unacceptable offering before the Lord, he did not receive God's favor. In contrast, Abel brought the prescribed offering and received God's favor. Cain was angry and downcast—he coveted the favor his brother had received (Gen 4:3-5). His covetous condition caused him to commit murder.

These Bible references are just a few of the many we could examine to understand that humanity was aware of God's Law well before He wrote it in stone. A careful study of Scripture should correct the false theology that the Ten Commandments didn't exist before Mt. Sinai.

Centuries before Moses was born, God judged men and women by the standard of whether they "obeyed My voice and kept My charge, My commandments, My statutes, and My laws" (Gen 26:4-5).

The Ten Commandments are God's ten "life principles." The sins recorded in the Scriptures are the breaking of these commandments. God has never used another set of laws by which He judged His people. Throughout the Bible, He judged those who kept the Ten Commandments as "righteous," while those who knowingly broke His Ten Commandments He declared as wicked sinners.

The early patriarchs—including Abraham, the father of faith—knew the requirements of God's Ten Commandment Law.

Can we also find evidence all Ten Commandments remained in force in the New Testament? Yes, we can! Most Christians readily agree the New Testament recounts nine of the ten as binding today. Controversy seems to revolve around only the Fourth Commandment—keeping holy the seventh-day (Saturday) Sabbath of God.

Since that's where the disagreement begins, that's where we'll begin. Let's first review a few facts from the New Testament, and then we'll take a closer look at this issue in the following chapters.

A resurrected Savior appointed Paul to be an apostle. On what day did Paul worship God? "And he reasoned in the synagogue every Sabbath, and persuaded both Jews and Greeks" (Acts 18:4). Here we see both Jews and Gentiles kept the Sabbath of the Lord (*see also* Acts 13:14, 42). More importantly, we see the converted Paul keeping the weekly seventh-day Sabbath well after the resurrection of our Lord.

As we will soon study, not one single Scripture in the Bible indicates that God transferred the sanctity of His seventh-day (Saturday) Sabbath to the first day of the week. In contrast to a popular teaching, we'll let New Testament Scripture prove that none of the early Christians observed Sunday as the weekly day of worship.

The New Testament records a number of disputes between Christian converts of Jewish heritage and those who came from the Gentile heritage. Some within the fellowship were identified as "Judaizers," those who were keen on insisting the ceremonial laws of Moses be maintained.

Great disputes broke out between these Judaizers and the new believers over days observed for "fasting," whether Gentiles should be circumcised, whether the annual sabbath days should be celebrated, and more. But you won't find one single argument over the weekly seventh-day Sabbath of God as the day of worship. They all worshiped on God's holy Sabbath day, and none questioned that it was the seventh day of the week (Saturday).

If there were no other indicators about New Testament Sabbath-keeping, this would be enough to convince me that God's appointed day of weekly worship remains. I realize this line of reasoning isn't persuasive enough for most, so let me whet your appetite with a few more New Testament texts.

"So He came to Nazareth, where He had been brought up. And as His custom was, He went into the synagogue on the Sabbath day, and stood up to read" (Lk 4:16). It was the custom of Jesus to keep the seventh-day Sabbath. You might think, *"Sure, that's because He was still living in the Jewish economy."*

Yet, in three and one-half years of ministry, not once did Jesus even hint to His disciples that the Sabbath would be altered. In fact, when He prophesied about the destruction of Jerusalem which would occur in A.D. 70 (nearly four decades after His ascension to heaven), He acknowledged the Sabbath would still remain in force (Mt 24:20).

There are numerous texts about keeping the Ten Commandment Law of God in the New Testament. Jesus never deleted a single commandment—only man has tried to do that.

Did you know the New Testament actually declares that there "remains a Sabbath-keeping" of God's holy day after the resurrection? Let me show you: "For if Joshua had given them rest *[Greek: katapauo]*, then He would not afterward have spoken of another day. There remains therefore a rest *[Greek: sabbatismos]* for the people of God" (Heb 4:8-9).

Joshua led the stiff-necked people of God into the Promised Land. Still, he could not *restrain them to physical rest*, which is the meaning of the Greek word *katapauo*. So the Bible tells us that there *remains* a *sabbatismos* rest for the people of God.

To "remain" implies it existed before. The literal translation of the Greek word *sabbatismos* is "Sabbath-keeping." There remains a Sabbath-keeping blessing for Christians today! A day when we cease from all of our works, as God did from His.

God purposed the seventh-day (Saturday) Sabbath to be both a physical and spiritual rest—a day to focus entirely on Him, trusting in His salvation. God intended His weekly Sabbath to be a blessing in our lives, a time when we could come apart and be exclusively with Him. God desired and designed our weekly Sabbath observance to be our delight (Is 58:13-14).

It amazes me how mixed-up our thinking has become. Many people today consider keeping all of the Ten Commandments as "being under bondage." That certainly wasn't the Apostle Paul's attitude. "… The law *is* holy, and the commandment holy and just and good. … For I delight in the law of God according to the inward man" (Rom 7:12, 22).

It wasn't the psalmist's state of mind either. "Great peace have those who love Your law, and nothing causes them to stumble. … I long for Your salvation, O LORD, and Your law *is* my delight" (Ps 119:165, 174).

And James referred to the Ten Commandments as the "law of liberty," saying if we continue in them—as doers of the work—we'll be blessed in whatever we do (Ja 1:25).

Where there is no law, there is no sin. Genesis records many accounts of breaking the principles of the Ten Commandments. It also records God's judgments on those who committed the sin. Do you recall the Bible definition for sin? Sin is the transgression, or breaking of, God's Law (1 John 3:4).

Doesn't the New Testament make it clear that to avoid sin we should avoid breaking the Ten Commandment Law? "For whoever shall keep the whole law, and yet stumble in one *point*, he is guilty of all. For He who said, 'Do not commit adultery,' also said, 'Do not murder.' Now if you do not commit adultery, but you do murder, you have become a transgressor of the law" (Ja 2:10-11).

The New Testament establishes Abraham's true descendants are those who belong to Christ. As Abraham's descendants, we are heirs according to the covenant made with him (Gal 3:29). Our belief and faith in Christ as our Savior credits us with His righteousness—hallelujah!

Are we then expected to conform to God's divine will and the pattern of Christ's obedience to maintain our upright relationship with Him?

"If you know that He is righteous, you know that everyone who practices righteousness is born of Him" (1 Jn 2:29). God warns us not to be deceived today, because "only he who practices righteousness is righteous" (1 Jn 3:7). The righteousness of Christ and the Holy Spirit within us empower us to walk according to God's standards.

God inspired David to write—"The law of the LORD *is* perfect, converting the soul ..." (Ps 19:7). It was an awe-inspiring event when the Lord spoke His perfect Ten Commandment Law to the assembly of Israel! You might want to review Exodus, chapters 19 and 20, to contemplate what the people experienced.

If God purposed to alter His "perfect" law, He certainly would not have done it in an understated manner. Jesus would have proclaimed it from the top of His lungs! Instead, this is what Christ said—

"For assuredly, I say to you, till heaven and earth pass away, one jot or one tittle will by no means pass from the law till all is fulfilled. Whoever therefore breaks one of the least of these commandments, and teaches men so, shall be called least in the kingdom of heaven; but whoever does and teaches them, he shall be called great in the kingdom of heaven" (Mt 5:18-19).

Jesus also said, "If you love Me, keep My commandments" (Jn 14:15). Love compels Christians who learn the truth about the Law of God to keep all of the Ten Commandments. We don't keep them *to be* saved. We keep them because we *are* saved. Faith and works are not at odds with each other—they go hand-in-glove together.

If we search the Scriptures, rightly dividing the word of God, we'll find God's Ten Commandments in force from Genesis to Revelation. As we studied in chapter three, the Law of Moses was the "temporary, Old Covenant" with the children of Israel.

The eternal Ten Commandment Law was included in both the Old and New Covenants. God's Law served as His standard of judgment before Mt. Sinai and continued to do so after the resurrection.

6

The Lords Day

The Bible leaves no doubt which day belongs to our Lord. All Scriptures that define the Lord's *special day* assign the honor to Saturday, the seventh day of the week. Does that surprise you?

Did you know there is no Bible reference to the *first day of the week* as being the Lord's Day? Not one single Scripture makes that connection. In this chapter, we'll examine each Bible verse that speaks of "the first day of the week."

Don't worry, it won't be cumbersome—there are only eight (five of which refer to the same event). First, let's consider how this error crept into the church.

Most Christian churches base their doctrines (teachings) on Bible texts. *Sound* biblical doctrines are developed from an in-depth study of all Scriptures related to a certain topic—examined within their recorded context. But people hatch *unsound* doctrines when they take the haphazard approach of using only a few Scriptures—taken out of context.

One widely accepted doctrine goes beyond *unsound* to the point of *unreasonable*. This teaching has absolutely *no Scripture* to support it. It's a tradition of man practiced by Catholics and most Protestants.

That tradition substitutes "Sunday-keeping" in place of keeping God's seventh-day (Saturday) Sabbath commandment. In chapter seven we will trace the origin and history of this custom, which the Catholic Church claims to have instigated and handed down as their "mark of authority" to change the Word of God.

"*All too* well you reject the commandment of God, that you may keep your tradition ... making the word of God of no effect through your tradition which you have handed down ..." (Mk 7:9, 13).

With those words, Jesus rebuked the Pharisees of His day. Do Christians who keep man's tradition of *Sunday worship* hear the echo of Christ's reprimand?

Christians are trampling on the Day of the Lord! Most aren't aware they are trespassing on holy ground. "If you turn away your foot from the Sabbath, from doing your pleasure on My holy day, and call the Sabbath a delight, the holy day of the LORD honorable ... Then you shall delight yourself in the LORD ..." (Is 58:13-14).

Did you notice that God claims the seventh-day Sabbath as "My holy day ... the holy day of the Lord"? We are stepping over the authority of the Lord when we do not turn away our feet from trampling on His holy day.

"... The seventh day *is* the Sabbath of the LORD your God" (Ex 20:10). The seventh day belongs to God. It is the Lord's Day.

According to the Bible, all things were created through Christ—nothing was made without Him (Jn 1:3). Just after Christ created man, He made the Sabbath for man's benefit. Jesus proclaimed His Lordship over this holy seventh day, "Therefore the Son of Man is also Lord of the Sabbath" (Mk 2:28).

How could so many Christians be deceived into dismissing the holy Sabbath of God and substituting another day by tradition? How was this false alternative to God's system of government planted? I can't assume what I've written so far will erase the deception, because this error is now too deeply rooted within the Christian community.

If you're not already obeying the fourth commandment, you probably have a number of questions that I have yet to answer. For that reason, I invite you to journey with me to the end of this book. I've dedicated a number of chapters to answering the questions that I think may be lingering in your mind.

Let's set the fourth commandment of God on the shelf for just a moment. Without this commandment to remember the seventh-day (Saturday) Sabbath and keep it holy, there is *no earthly reason* that sets Saturday apart as special. Actually, without that commandment, there is *no earthly reason for our weekly cycle of time.* It has nothing to do with the positioning of the sun, or the orbiting and rotation of the earth and our moon.

From the physical perspective, why don't we have five or ten days in our week? What difference would it make which day we keep holy? What advantage would there be to worshiping and resting on Saturday, versus Sunday or any other day of the week?

Why does the whole world keep a seven-day weekly cycle? There's *no earthly reason* I can think of.

Ah—but there is *a heavenly reason!* God established and set apart the weekly cycle of time by the authority of His Word alone. Just after He created man, God decreed the seven-day division—

"And on the seventh day God ended His work which He had done, and He rested on the seventh day from all His work which He had done. Then God blessed the seventh day and sanctified it, because in it He rested from all His work which God had created and made" (Gen 2:2-3).

It was God Who inspired Moses to write "seventh day" not once, but *three times* in that passage. Why is the seventh day the last day of our weekly cycle? Because God determined it to be a day of rest, a holy intermission.

There's only one reason the seventh-day (Saturday) Sabbath is holy—God *blessed and sanctified* that particular day and called it "My holy day." That's reason enough for me. How about you?

But how can we explain the Apostle John's comment from Revelation? When John received the Revelation of Jesus Christ he wrote, "I, John … was on the island that is called Patmos for the word of God and for the testimony of Jesus Christ. I was in the Spirit on the Lord's Day, and I heard behind me a loud voice, as of a trumpet" (Rev 1:9-10).

What was the "Lord's Day" on which John received the revelation? Some people think John referred to the great, final day of the Lord (when God pours out His wrath on the earth). But notice that John described his location, his reason for being there, and his condition of "being in the Spirit" when he received this vision.

Doesn't it seem more likely that John spoke of the actual day he received the vision? Most Bible scholars hold to this interpretation.

John stated, "I was in the Spirit on the Lord's Day." In the Greek, it literally translates "the day of the Lord." There's no reference to the first day of the week, Sunday. So where did that idea originate?

In the Roman Empire, the first day of the week (Sunday) was called "the Lord's [Emperor's] Day" because Sunday was the day the emperor received his treasury payments. Sun-worshiping pagans also celebrated Sunday as "the venerable day of the Sun."

The Romans had banished John to the lonely isle of Patmos for his testimony of Jesus. Do you think John would acknowledge Sunday, the *Lord's Day* honoring the Roman Emperor or the *Day of the Sun*, as the day of his Lord?

John kept the Sabbath with Jesus. He knew God called the seventh-day Sabbath "MY HOLY DAY." He was there when

Christ proclaimed to be Lord of the Sabbath. As a committed disciple of Jesus, doesn't it seem logical that "the day of the Lord" to John could mean nothing else than God's seventh-day (Saturday) Sabbath?

Many people think Sunday is called "the Lord's Day" because Christ was resurrected on the first day of the week. It's obvious that Christians eventually labeled Sunday as such. But that didn't occur until some time in the last part of the second century—at least seventy-five years after John wrote the book of Revelation.

When I checked *Strong's Concordance* for their reference to the Lord's Day, it read "… the day of the Lord, what we commonly call Sunday." *Strong's* typically provides a list of Scriptures related to a given topic. Here they listed nothing further than the single reference to John's Patmos isle statement in Revelation 1:10. And for good reason!

The only Scriptures defining a day that God calls His own refer to the seventh day, never the first. I challenge you to study this topic in depth. If you find any biblical evidence contrary to what I've written, please let me know. I've studied from Genesis to Revelation on this subject and I can't find a single Bible text to suggest Sunday is the Lord's Day.

As Creator God of the universe, the Lord exercises ownership of each day. But there is only one day that He claims to be blessed and sanctified as His special day of the week—the seventh-day (Saturday) Sabbath.

Do you still cling to the thought that Paul said we should not allow men to judge us regarding seventh-day Sabbath-keeping? Let's review his comment and see if we can interpret his meaning beyond question—

"So let no one judge you in food or in drink, or regarding a festival or a new moon or sabbaths, which are a shadow of things to come, but the substance is of Christ" (Col 2:16-17).

It's critical to examine this verse in the context of Paul's writing to understand which sabbaths were the subject. He was teaching that the *"handwriting of ordinances"* was nailed to the cross (Col 2:14) and those requirements had been eliminated.

The Law of Moses decreed annual ceremonial sabbaths during the great festivals that were symbolic of the ministry of Christ. Do you know what governed the celebration of these annual sabbaths? The Book of the Law set forth specific instructions for these ceremonial days—many detailed ordinances regarding food, drink, and other observances.

These special annual sabbath days were merely shadows of salvation to point people to Jesus. Christ was the substance, or the Body that cast the shadow. For this reason, two verses later, Paul said don't allow a man to judge you regarding food or drink, and the keeping of the annual ceremonial sabbaths. Do you see that he definitely was not referring to the seventh-day Sabbath of the fourth commandment?

Now, let's take the fourth commandment off the shelf and put it back where it belongs, as part of the total package of God's Ten Commandments.

The frailty of our human reasoning might not comprehend why God wants us to worship on the seventh day of the week. As I said, there's *no earthly reason for Saturday to be more special than any other day of the week.* It doesn't make sense to us. But if we ignore the Scriptures and refuse to obey the commandment of God, we are calling God's authority into question!

The seventh-day Sabbath is the day God set aside for church services. "Six days shall work be done, but the seventh day *is* a Sabbath of solemn rest, a holy convocation. You shall do no work *on it*; it *is* the Sabbath of the LORD in all your dwellings" (Lev 23:3).

The seventh-day (Saturday) Sabbath is a call from God for a holy convocation—a summons to meet together in a sacred assembly to worship our Lord. Jesus established the pattern for us to follow. "... And as His custom was, He went into the synagogue on the Sabbath day" (Lk 4:16).

Some people think there is proof in the New Testament that the disciples worshiped on the first day of the week after the crucifixion of Jesus. There are only eight times in the entire Bible when the phrase "first day of the week" appears, and each reference is in the New Testament (the seventh-day Sabbath is mentioned 59 times in the New Testament alone).

Before we discuss the "first day of the week" verses, it will be helpful to review the definition of a day in accordance with Bible times. "God called the light Day, and the darkness He called Night. So the evening and the morning were the first day" (Gen 1:5).

A Bible day began at evening sunset. A clear practice of this time-keeping method is found in Leviticus 23:32, "... From evening to evening, you shall celebrate your sabbath."

The weekly Sabbath observance was from Friday sunset to Saturday sunset. Although Romans calculated time as we do today (with a new day beginning at midnight), Jesus' disciples defined the *beginning* of their day as *the period that followed sunset.*

Five of the eight Bible references to the "first day of the week" (Mt 28:1; Mk 16:2; Mk 16:9; Lk 24:1; Jn 20:1) correspond with the day when Christ's women disciples returned to His tomb on resurrection morning.

It's interesting to note that after the crucifixion, these devoted disciples of Christ first "rested on the Sabbath according to the commandment" (Lk 23:56). Although they were anxious to anoint His dead body with spices and fragrant oils, they waited from late Friday afternoon to early Sunday morning to return to His grave. They obviously knew the Sabbath commandment wasn't abolished at the cross.

Now let's take a brief look at the other three references of the "first day of the week."

First is John 20:19, where we find the trembling disciples of Christ assembled on the first day of the week, resurrection Sunday. Following the crucifixion, they were huddled together behind doors barred shut for fear of the Jews. How could anyone believe this was a worship service?

The disciples did not yet understand that Christ would be resurrected from His grave. They didn't believe the report of those to whom Jesus had already appeared—the women disciples and the men who returned after their encounter with Christ on the road to Emmaus. This gathering started as a solemn and fearful event. You can read Mark 16:12-14 and Luke 24:33-49 for more background information on this event.

In the second reference, Acts 20:7, the disciples were gathered together to break bread with Paul for his final farewell meeting before he departed on his journey. Luke records this was on the "first day of the week," beginning at sunset on Saturday. It appears Paul had a lot to say in his farewell message. He prolonged his sermon until midnight.

Poor Eutychus nodded off during the sermon and fell from the third floor to his death. Many believe the only reason Luke recorded this incident was because God performed a miracle through Paul and brought the young man back to life. Then Paul continued talking until Sunday morning, daylight of the first day of the week.

The third reference to the "first day of the week" (other than those mentioned in the Gospel of Christ's resurrection day), is found in 1 Corinthians 16:2. In that verse, Paul instructs the brethren to systematically store up a collection for the benefit of famine stricken believers in Jerusalem, by *laying aside* something on the first day of each week.

The literal Greek translation is to "lay by him in store"— which translated means to treasure it up "by himself," "in his home." Paul wanted the contributions to be ready when he arrived, so he could forward the goods to the church in Jerusalem by representatives. This is hardly a reference to Sunday-keeping as the day of worship.

Other than references to Christ's day of resurrection, only three Scriptures refer to the "first day of the week." We've just reviewed them. Do you see any evidence that God transferred His holy day from Saturday to Sunday?

Since God placed such importance on His holy Sabbath day, it only makes sense that He would have announced any change to His day of worship in some spectacular fashion. Don't you agree? Can you imagine Him silently sweeping this commandment under the rug and leaving it for man to *guess* or *speculate* about His will?

Sunday-keeping is a tradition of man. Most Bible scholars readily admit that. We'll look at their commentaries in chapter seven.

I've met many people who agree that we need to set apart some time for God and rest one day in seven. Still, they say it doesn't make any difference which day we choose, as long as we rest. What a slap in the face this must be to our Creator God!

It's a classic example of created beings thinking they are smarter than the Creator. In this case, the "created" are telling the Creator that He had no right to authorize the day of worship and rest. God's commands don't always compute with our *little finite minds*, but that doesn't negate our obligation to obey Almighty God.

Through the years, many well-meaning Christians have tried to discourage me from keeping the Bible Sabbath. They speak in excited tones of "legalism, bondage, Jewish tradition" and such. But I've never known one of these to claim that keeping the other nine Commandments falls into these categories.

Can you imagine what that would sound like? "Oh, you're under the bondage of a Jewish tradition if you take God's commandment not to murder seriously. You're nothing but a legalist." Would they think I was under bondage because I don't bow down to graven images and have other *gods* before my Creator God? Keeping the Sabbath is all about enjoying an intimate relationship with God. It's about freedom, not bondage.

Then there are those who quote Ephesians 2:8, saying with great enthusiasm we are saved by grace alone, through faith. Absolutely—I agree! Still, have they not read the two verses beyond that, where Paul said that we were "created in Christ Jesus for good works, which God prepared beforehand that we should walk in them" (Eph 2:10)?

Or how about James 2:20, "faith without works is dead"? Better yet, have they never read Hebrews 5:9, which affirms that Christ "became the author of eternal salvation to all who obey Him"?

Did Paul believe since we're saved by grace, through faith, that we could ignore God's Ten Commandment Law? "Therefore by the deeds of the law no flesh will be justified in His sight, for by the law *is* the knowledge of sin. ... Do we then make void the law through faith? Certainly not! On the contrary, we establish the law" (Rom 3:20, 31).

The Greek definition for *establish* is "to cause it to stand." Apart from Jesus Christ, we can do nothing! It is only by the transforming power of His life and His Spirit in us that we can keep God's Ten Commandments.

In Hebrews 8:10, the writer repeated God's promise of the New Covenant from Jeremiah 31:33, "I will put My laws in their mind and write them on their hearts; and I will be their God, and they shall be My people." It is by faith the Ten Commandments of God are established in our hearts.

It is faith and absolute trust in God that causes the Sabbath to stand as a memorial to our Creator. Every seventh-day Sabbath turns our thoughts back to creation—to the One Who first created humanity in His image, and now is recreating us in His image. By faith, we look back to the day God set aside the Sabbath as a memorial of His creation (Gen 2:2-3).

God knew the pressures of our workweek would entangle us in earthly matters, and we would forget to acknowledge Him as our all-powerful Creator. He established the weekly Sabbath to return our thoughts to Him, to give us spiritual encouragement, physical rest, and hope in the future.

Every seventh-day Sabbath we can rest from the burdens of this world and focus on our God. We are mindful that greater is He Who lives in us, than he who is in the world (1 Jn 4:4).

"Surely My Sabbaths you shall keep, for it is a sign between Me and you throughout your generations, that *you* may know that I *am* the LORD who sanctifies you. You shall keep the Sabbath, therefore, for *it is* holy to you" (Ex 31:13-14).

It is by faith that we keep God's seventh-day Sabbath as a memorial that God is the One Who is sanctifying us—equipping us and making us holy (*see also* Ezek 20:12). We accept, by faith, that He Who has begun a good work in us will be faithful to complete it (Phil 1:6).

There is *no earthly reason* to keep the fourth commandment of God. But there is the greatest *spiritual reason* in the entire created universe. The seventh-day (Saturday) Sabbath is the mark of God's authority as Creator and Redeemer! He calls it His *sign* between us that He is the One Who sanctifies us.

Are we really willing to trust and obey God? The Sabbath is a *sign* of our allegiance. It demonstrates whether we are serving God, our Creator—or man, who dismisses the Lord's commandment by tradition.

Will Christians recognize God's mark of authority, or continue to allow tradition to take precedence over His Holy Word?

"'For as the new heavens and the new earth which I will make shall remain before Me,' says the LORD, 'So shall your descendants and your name remain. And it shall come to pass *that* … from one Sabbath to another, all flesh shall come to worship before Me,' says the LORD" (Is 66:22-23).

The sacred Sabbath is perpetual! We will be celebrating the Lord's Day throughout eternity. Why should we allow an unsound doctrine, a tradition of man that has no scriptural basis, to steal our joy now?

God sanctified the seventh day of each week for our benefit, so we could spend special time with Him and rest from all our worldly concerns.

The seventh-day Sabbath is the only day God defines as "My holy day"—the Lord's Day.

7

Made For Man

*T*he Sabbath was made for man, and not man for the Sabbath" (Mk 2:27). What did Jesus mean? It helps to see the literal translation of Jesus' comment—"the Sabbath was made for the sake of mankind."

God is the giver of every good and perfect gift. In His love for us, the Lord established the Sabbath for our benefit. God first created man, and then He crowned His creation by ordaining His eternal Sabbath. This was His act of love to bless us!

The Lord assigned such special significance to His holy day that it became the heart of the Law. But the Pharisees robbed the weekly Sabbath of its intended joy by imposing somber rituals and banning thirty-nine routine tasks. According to their manufactured rules, a person was guilty of Sabbath-breaking if he simply tied or untied a knot, or ate an egg laid on the Sabbath!

With such ridiculous restrictions, Sabbath-keeping became a burden of pettiness rather than a blessing of praise. And, as you might guess, in the natural decline of man's reasoning, people began to plot and scheme. Soon they devised ways to get around the extended requirements, while satisfying the "letter" of the man-made regulations. Sadly, the spirit of Sabbath celebration was lost.

"Therefore the Son of Man is also Lord of the Sabbath" (Mk 2:28). Christ was Master of the Sabbath—not a slave to it, as the Pharisees promoted. Jesus refused to comply with the restrictions that caused controversy on His holy day. He announced His Lordship even of the Sabbath day and His authority to reinstate the spiritual purposes that He originally intended.

What were His reasons for instituting the Sabbath? I found this quote in *Easton's Illustrated Dictionary.* I couldn't word it any better, so here it is—

"The Sabbath, originally instituted for man at his creation, is of permanent and universal obligation. The physical necessities of man require a Sabbath of rest. He is so constituted that his bodily welfare needs at least one day in seven for rest from ordinary labour. Experience also proves that the moral and spiritual necessities of men also demand a Sabbath of rest."

Easton's went on to quote F. W. Robertson (1816-1853), a Christian revivalist sometimes known as the Victorian conscience—

"I am more and more sure by experience that the reason for the observance of the Sabbath lies deep in the everlasting necessities of human nature, and that as long as man is man the blessedness of keeping it, not as a day of rest only, but as a day of spiritual rest, will never be annulled. I certainly do feel by experience the eternal obligation, because of the eternal necessity, of the Sabbath.

"The soul withers without it. It thrives in proportion to its observance. The Sabbath was made for man. God made it for men in a certain spiritual state because they needed it. The need, therefore, is deeply hidden in human nature. He who can dispense with it must be holy and spiritual indeed. And he who, still unholy and unspiritual, would yet dispense with it is a man that would fain be wiser than his Maker."

The Lord established the Sabbath as a taste of heavenly rest. For knowing Him more intimately, God ordained one day in seven for us to unite without the usual daily distractions. He desires our weekly Sabbath celebration to be a memorial day, reminding us that He is not only our Creator, but also our Redeemer.

The design of the Sabbath demonstrates our total dependence upon the One Who loves us with an everlasting love. As we enter into His rest each week in this special manner, God causes us to recognize the work He will do in us, to sanctify us by His power. He wants us to recognize that He will empower us to walk in obedience, motivated by our love for Him.

Sabbath-keeping is all about relationship with a loving God! Think about it. The essence of what Our Creator God is saying to us is something like this—

"I have chosen a special day in the week to spend entirely with you. I have blessed it and sanctified it. This is My holy day—set apart for our special time together. I will cause you to forget all the things that Satan is doing to 'steal, kill and destroy' you. Come apart from your earthly concerns. Come rest in Me.

"Join Me in this special day so that we may celebrate our relationship. As you abide in My Presence, your depression and discouragement will vanish. I will lift you this day to spiritual heights that look beyond this world. I will restore your joy. I will fill you to overflowing with hope. I will cause a peace that transcends all understanding to wash over you. Come, My child, for I love you and I want to spend this time with you."

How exciting it was for me to discover that God made the Sabbath *for* me! Unfortunately, the church congregation of my youth had legalistic tendencies toward Sabbath-keeping—placing their focus on a list of what *not* to do, rather than the joy of what we *could* do.

My parents adopted that same attitude and I suffered through the stifling limitations of many Sabbaths. In later years, my deepening relationship with God and His Word shed some much-needed light on the subject.

When I learned the Sabbath was God's expression of love for me, it made a dramatic difference in my Sabbath observance. No longer was it an attempt to appease God by my obedience. Rather, I drew nearer to spend time with Him on His holy seventh-day Sabbaths, as my expression of love for Him.

Here's the testimony of my co-author about discovering the Sabbath truth—

"I grew up in a family that demanded perfection from me. The church I attended as a youth painted a picture of a wrathful God who also demanded perfection. I thought the Heavenly Father was watching over me, ready to zap me when I missed the mark.

"All of my life I was performing for acceptance—for my family's and my God's. It wasn't until the Lord taught me His Sabbath truth that I was cut free from the cord of this performance mentality.

"The first time I ever experienced complete *freedom from performance* was on the first Sabbath I celebrated. I sensed I had been given permission to sit back, relax and enjoy—no work, no daily duties, no demands. But most of all, I had the whole day to spend with God.

"I suddenly knew *that I knew* He would sanctify me—causing me to be all that He called me to be. Talk about entering into His rest! There is nothing like it! That's why Exodus 31:13 is my favorite Scripture about the Sabbath. It's a sign for me to remember that it is God Who works in me to sanctify me—developing Christ's character of holiness.

"Still, towards the end of the week, I sometimes find

I'm slipping back into a *performance mentality*—thinking I'm not doing enough for God. But as I welcome the Sabbath, God reminds me of Galatians 3:3, 'Are you so foolish? Having begun in the Spirit, are you now being made perfect by the flesh?' The Sabbath reminds me that apart from Christ, I can do nothing.

"My life experience with God went through a radical transformation when I began celebrating His seventh-day Sabbath. I became aware that His grace is sufficient—His power is made perfect in my weakness.

"I learned obedience is the pathway to blessing. And it's so much easier to obey, now that I know to depend totally upon Him for all things. Celebrating the Sabbath has taught me to receive God's love in a new dimension."

Now that's the reason God instituted the Sabbath! When God finished His work of creation, He ceased His labor to celebrate! "God *blessed* the seventh day and *sanctified* it ..." (Gen 2:3).

The Hebrew word for *sanctified* is "qadas," and it appears for the first time in the Bible in Genesis 2:3. Qadas (sanctified) means "to declare something holy or to declare it to be used exclusively for celebrating God's glory" (*Vine's Expository Dictionary of Old and New Testament Words*).

The seventh day was set apart from the other days of the week, declared to be *holy* and to be used *wholly* for His glory! "For the sake of mankind" God ordained the Sabbath at Creation. Adam and Eve were the only humans on earth at the time. God created a special day each week to celebrate with His new family—to develop the relationship between God and man more fully.

I don't understand why Christians balk at believing God instituted the Sabbath at creation. They don't take that attitude about marriage. Most Christians acknowledge that God established the sanctity of marriage in the Garden of Eden.

In the same way He "blessed the seventh day and sanctified it," He also blessed and sanctified the marriage of Adam to Eve. He instituted marriage on the spot. "Therefore a man shall leave his father and mother and be joined to his wife, and they shall become one flesh" (Gen 2:24).

Have you ever heard anyone claim that the institution of marriage wasn't in force until Mt. Sinai, or that marriage was only for the Jews? Sounds rather ridiculous, doesn't it?

From the record of Adam and Eve's marriage until Mt. Sinai, you won't find another explicit command regarding marriage. Yet, in the New Testament, God's words from that first marriage ceremony are repeated or referred to on three occasions (Mk 10:8; 1 Cor 6:16; Eph 5:31).

The entire Christian world affirms that marriage was God's gift to us at creation. Why don't they apply that same power of reasoning to the Sabbath? Why should we assume the first married couple didn't continue to enjoy the blessed and sanctified day of the Lord each week?

It was with first-hand knowledge that Jesus spoke of the Sabbath being made "for the sake of mankind." The Father, Son, and Holy Spirit worked together in creation. Christ knew He blessed and sanctified the seventh day as a special gift for His created beings. He made it for man—not for Himself. And nothing remotely suggests that He put the Sabbath on hold until the time of Moses and the Jewish nation.

We must remember that although God made an eternal covenant of *salvation by grace through faith* with Abraham, He confirmed the covenant with the patriarch's son because "Abraham obeyed My voice and kept My charge, My commandments, My statutes, and My laws" (Gen 26:5). That is a statement of completeness. Throughout the Bible, Scripture links all these descriptions to God's Ten Commandment Moral Law.

God keeps covenant with those who keep covenant with Him—with those who love Him and keep His commandments (Deut 7:9, Dan 9:4, Neh 1:5).

There is no logical reason for anyone to assume the commandments Abraham kept differed in any way from the ones God handed Moses on stone. How could an intellectually honest person claim the set of laws that Abraham, Isaac, and Jacob obeyed didn't include the Sabbath commandment?

I also encourage you to remember how God dealt with Israel. When Israel went down to Egypt, only seventy persons joined Joseph there. During the time they remained in Egypt, God made them "as the stars of heaven in multitude" (Deut 10:22). But what started as a bountiful haven soon turned into a bitter slave hole.

During four hundred years of captivity, the Pharaohs robbed Israel of the privilege to practice all of God's law as handed down by their ancestors. Even so, listen to what God told Moses in the desert, after He led them out of Egypt and prepared to rain manna from heaven on Israel—

"Behold, I will rain bread from heaven for you. And the people shall go out and gather a certain quota every day, that I may test them, whether they will walk in My law or not" (Ex 16:4). *The question is—what law did God refer to here?*

Moses explained it to the people when he said, "Six days you shall gather it, but on the seventh day, *which is* the Sabbath, there will be none." Some scoffed at Moses' instructions and went out to gather food on the seventh day, only to return disappointed with empty baskets.

Now consider the Lord's response, "How long do you refuse to keep My commandments and My laws? See! For the LORD has given you the Sabbath; therefore He gives you on the sixth day bread for two days. Let every man remain in his place; let no man go out of his place on the seventh day."

The people took God's displeasure over breaking His Sabbath Law seriously, and they began resting on the seventh day (Ex 16:26-30).

If you check the Exodus timeline, God required the Israelites He redeemed from bondage to keep His Sabbath Commandment well *before* they came to Mt. Sinai. It was after this incident that they received water from the rock, victory over the Amalekites, and Jethro advised Moses how to establish a governing system to ease the wearied leader. Some time later, they came to Mt. Sinai.

Since God expressed His desire to test "whether they will walk in My law or not" *before* Moses declared to them it was a Sabbath and *before* God gave the Ten Commandments at Mt. Sinai, then doesn't it stand to reason the holy Sabbath day instituted at creation was handed down from generation to generation?

The Bible says from one Sabbath to another throughout eternity, "all flesh" will worship before the Lord (Is 66:22-23). It makes sense that we'll have a weekly worship day in the new heavens and new earth—a day to congregate and fellowship with our Lord and each other, just as we do now.

What makes no sense at all, however, is why God would initially bless and sanctify the Sabbath, eliminate it for a period, reinstate it for the Jews, eliminate it again, and then reinstate it when *all flesh* were united after the resurrection of His people.

Doesn't it seem obviously consistent to believe the seventh-day Sabbath that God blessed and sanctified is a perpetual covenant of love with His people?

God reinforced His Commandments by writing them with His own finger on two stone tablets (the tablets of the Testimony). He then instructed they be stored in a permanent place, inside the ark of His covenant, His throne, in the Most Holy Place of the Temple.

Where do you think God's ark-throne is today? "Then the temple of God was opened in heaven, and the ark of His covenant was seen in His temple ..." (Rev 11:19). Don't you think the real ark in heaven has the same contents as the symbolic ark on earth that was built according to its pattern?

Of all considerations, this is what fascinates me most. When God wrote His Commandments on stone He started only the Fourth one (His seventh-day Sabbath) with the word "REMEMBER." Would somebody please explain to me why that is the only Commandment the Christian church wants to forget?

"For thus says the Lord GOD, the Holy One of Israel: 'In returning and rest you shall be saved; in quietness and confidence shall be your strength.' But you would not" (Is 30:15). My co-author claimed this verse as her *life verse* for many years. The irony is she never quoted the last four words "But you would not." She didn't realize what the Lord was trying to tell her in this verse until she celebrated her first Sabbath.

Let's review some of the Bible evidence we've studied so far to help explain why we should not forget what was created for our benefit, what God asked us to *remember—*

1. God instituted the Sabbath at Creation—He blessed and sanctified the seventh day. This is the only supporting reason for our weekly time cycle (Gen 2:2-3).
2. God made the Sabbath for the benefit of mankind (Mk 2:27). Adam and Eve were the only people in the Garden of Eden. If God made the Sabbath for them, they obviously observed and enjoyed their Sabbaths with Him. Most especially after their fateful fall. Sabbaths were the day they could cease from their sentence of hard labor and, once again, rest in their Redeemer.
3. Abraham and his descendants kept all of God's com-mandments, including the seventh-day Sabbath (Gen 26:4-5).

4. God required Moses and the children of Israel to keep His Sabbath law *before* He handed down the Ten Commandments (Ex 16:4, 26-30).

5. God reinforced His Ten Commandments—in stone, with His own finger—to magnify their divine moral priority to the children of Israel, who had lost evidence of their essential nature over four hundred years of captivity. He placed special emphasis on *remembering* His seventh-day Sabbath (Ex 20:8-11).

6. Jesus—King of kings and Lord of lords—provided a pattern for us. While on earth as *Son of Man,* He made it His *custom* to keep each Sabbath by attending worship services (Lk 4:16).

7. When Jesus prophesied about events that would take place forty years after His death (A.D. 70, the destruction of Jerusalem), He underscored the fact that His followers would still be observing His sacred weekly Sabbath day (Mt 24:20).

8. Jesus said He did not come to destroy the Law, but to fill it to the fullest spiritual meaning. He emphatically declared that not one "jot or tittle" would be changed until heaven and earth pass away (Mt 5:17-18).

9. Christ's disciples kept the Sabbath after the Crucifixion (Lk 23:56; Acts 13:14, 42-44; 16:13; 18:4). There's no mention in the New Testament (written up to sixty years after Christ's death) of changing or eliminating the seventh-day Sabbath.

10. The Old Covenant contained the Ten Commandments (Ex 24:4, 7-8; Deut 31:24-26).

11. The New Covenant contains the Ten Commandments (Jer 31:31-33; Heb 8:8, 10).

12. All flesh—all of God's redeemed people—will celebrate the Sabbath in the new heavens and new earth for all of eternity (Is 66:22-23).

It gives me a great deal of assurance to know that God does not change (Mal 3:6; Heb 13:8). One of the greatest life-lessons I have learned is that consistency in actions helps to develop trust, and if I can trust a person's word, I can trust that person.

God said, "My covenant I will not break, nor alter the word that has gone out of My lips" (Ps 89:34). I feel confident that God did not intend to change the Law that represented His nature of love and the expression of His perfect will. I also know beyond doubt that I can trust His word, because He never lies.

The Lord of the Sabbath promised to send us the Holy Spirit if we would walk in *covenant obedience* to Him. "If you love Me, keep My commandments. And I will pray the Father, and He will give you another Helper, that He may abide with you forever" (Jn 14:15-16).

Christ, our exalted Savior, gives repentance and forgiveness of sins. He also gives the Holy Spirit to those who obey Him—

"Him God has exalted to His right hand to be Prince and Savior, to give repentance to Israel and forgiveness of sins. And we are His witnesses to these things, and so also is the Holy Spirit whom God has given to those who obey Him" (Acts 5:31-32).

How well do we think we know this God of love, the holy and righteous Creator of the universe? If we claim to know Him without keeping His commandments, the Bible calls us a liar—

"He who says, 'I know Him,' and does not keep His commandments, is a liar, and the truth is not in him. But whoever keeps His word, truly the love of God is perfected in him. By this we know that we are in Him. He who says he abides in Him ought himself also to walk just as He walked" (1 Jn 2:4-6).

Do you earnestly want God to perfect His love in you? Is it the desire of your heart to abide in Christ and know the Lord *by personal experience*? Then, will you come to God with the same humble attitude of Christ?

"Behold, I come;
In the scroll of the book it is written of me.
I delight to do Your will, O my God;
Your Law is within my heart."
Psalms 40:7-8 NASB (see also Heb 10:7)

Will you take the Bible counsel to walk in the path of His footsteps, follow the Ten Commandments of God, and cherish the seventh-day (Saturday) Sabbath that He made especially for you?

The grace of Jesus Christ, the love of God, and the fellowship of the Holy Spirit will be poured out on you in a new and magnificent manner as you celebrate, each week, the day the Lord made for your benefit!

8

It's No Secret—Catholic Church Claims the Change

I consider myself a true Protestant. Since I don't know your persuasion, I want to make something clear at the onset of this chapter.

We will soon examine some claims and comments made public by the Catholic Church. I disagree with the position of authority on which this religious system thinks to stand. But I want to express my belief that God has His people in all churches—including the Roman Catholic Church.

God looks at the heart and judges people on an individual basis, according to their sincerity.

I have many wonderful Catholic friends who are dedicated Christians. I also have many sincere Christian friends who are Sunday-keeping Protestants. I don't agree with either group about the Sabbath issue, but God did not appoint me to judge any of them.

The purpose of this chapter is to present published claims of the Papal system regarding Sunday-keeping and Protestantism.

How much do you know about the Protestant Reformation? Sadly, most people of today's generation know very little. It had its roots in the late medieval age, when reformers John Wycliffe and Jan Hus confronted corruption within the Roman Catholic Church. But it was a Catholic monk by the name of Martin Luther who rocked the Papal system with reformation in the sixteenth century.

Tortured by uncertainty of God's love and his own salvation, Luther searched the Scriptures to resolve his spiritual crisis. He discovered the great Bible truths of justification and salvation by grace, through faith. Posting his *Ninety-five Theses* on the church door in Wittenberg, Luther sparked the Protestant Reformation that swept the land with shouts of "sola scriptura"—*the Bible and the Bible only!*

But, a breach of this *Bible only* doctrine has blurred the message of Protestantism. By historic definition, Protestants are those who protest the Pope's claim of ultimate authority over matters of religious faith. We are those who believe the Bible and accept its supreme authority as the Word of God.

At least, that's who we're supposed to be. But did you know that the Catholic Church chides Sunday-keeping Protestants for their lack of sticking with the Scriptures? Consider this quote from Reverend John O'Brien—

"But since Saturday, not Sunday, is specified [as the Sabbath of the Lord] in the Bible, isn't it curious that non-Catholics who profess to take their religion directly from the Bible and not from the church observe Sunday instead of Saturday? Yes, of course, it is inconsistent, but the change was made about fifteen centuries before Protestantism was born.

"They [Protestants] have continued to observe custom even though it rests upon the authority of the Catholic Church and not upon an explicit text in the Bible. That observance remains the reminder of the mother church from which non-Catholic sects broke away like a boy running away from his mother but still carrying in his pocket a picture of his mother or a lock of her hair" (*The Faith of Millions,* pp. 421, 422).

It's no secret! The Catholic Church claims to have transferred the sacredness of the seventh-day Saturday Sabbath to Sunday—

"Of course the Catholic Church claims that the change was her act. And the act is the mark of her ecclesiastical power and authority in religious matters" (*Faith of our Fathers,* p. 14, C. F. Thomas, Chancellor of Cardinal Gibbons). This is widely taught in their catechism and other Church documents.

We'll take a brief look at a few Catholic comments in a moment. But first, I have a few questions. Do they have a right to make that claim? Does the Papal system have the power to change God's commandments? Is it true Christians worship on Sunday based on the word of the Pope only?

Most Protestant laymen I have spoken with believe there must be some scriptural authority for keeping Sunday as though it was the Sabbath of the Lord. Even some pastors I have met make a transparently feeble claim to Bible support. Of course, you already know my position on this matter, but let me share commentary from other denominational leaders.

The great Baptist leader, Dr. E. T. Hiscox, authored the "Baptist Manual." Here is what he had to say about the Sabbath—

"There was and is a command to keep holy the Sabbath day, but that Sabbath day was not Sunday. It will however be readily said, and with some show of triumph, that the Sabbath was transferred from the seventh to the first day of the week, with all its duties, privileges and sanctions.

"Earnestly desiring information on this subject, which I have studied for many years, I ask, where can the record of such a transaction be found? Not in the New Testament, absolutely not. There is no scriptural evidence of the change of the Sabbath institution from the seventh to the first day of the week."

In a sermon at the Baptist Minister's Convention, Dr. Hiscox made these statements—

"To me it seems unaccountable that Jesus, during three years discussion with His disciples, often conversing with them upon the Sabbath question, discussing it in some of its various aspects, freeing it from its false (Jewish traditional) glosses, never alluded to any transference of the day: also, that during the forty days of His resurrection life, no such thing was intimated.

"Nor, so far as we know, did the Spirit, which was given to bring to their remembrance all things whatsoever that he had said unto them, deal with this question. Nor yet did the inspired apostles, in preaching the gospel, founding churches, counseling and instructing those founded, discuss or approach the subject.

"Of course I quite well know that Sunday did come into use in early Christian history as a religious day, as we learn from the Christians Fathers and other sources. But what a pity that is comes branded with the mark of paganism, and christened with the name of the sun-god, then adopted and sanctified by the papal apostasy, and bequeathed as a sacred legacy to Protestantism" (*New York Examiner,* Nov. 16, 1893).

You might find it interesting to read other denominational documents on this issue. Our Catholic friends have a website that publishes various Protestant statements that support the seventh-day Sabbath—Baptist, Methodist, Presbyterian, Episcopalian, Lutheran Free Church, Anglican, Disciples of Christ, Congregationalist and many others.

They are too numerous to list, but in a moment I'll provide the information for you to access these on the website, MaryOnLine. I appreciated this quote that was short enough to include—

"The sacred name of the Seventh day is Sabbath. This fact is too clear to require argument ... (Ex 20:10 quoted). ... On this point the plain teaching of the Word has been admitted in all ages. ... Not once did the disciples apply the Sabbath law to the first day of the week—that folly was left for a later age, nor did they pretend that the first day supplanted the seventh" (Southern Baptist Joseph Judson Taylor, *The Sabbath Question,* pp. 14-17, 41).

Folly indeed! Do you realize God put His seal of authority on His holy seventh-day Sabbath? Just as an earthly monarch's seal includes reference to their name, title and dominion, God included these references in His fourth commandment—

"Remember the Sabbath day, to keep it holy. ... The seventh day *is* the Sabbath of the LORD your God. ... For *in* six days the LORD made the heavens and the earth, the sea, and all that *is* in them, and rested the seventh day. Therefore the LORD blessed the Sabbath day and hallowed it" (Ex 20:8-11). God placed His "mark" on the Sabbath.

The very name "Sabbath" bears God's mark of authority. The Hebrew word for Sabbath is *Shabbath.* Let's break it down in the Hebrew and see the statement God made about His holy day—

Sha means *eternal one. Ab,* the root word of *Abba,* means *Father. Bath or Beth* means *house of* or *sign of.* Combined as *Shabbath* they pack a powerful testimony—*Sign of the eternal Father.*

"Surely My Sabbaths you shall keep, for it *is* a **sign** between Me and you throughout your generations, that *you* may know that I *am* the LORD who sanctifies you" (Ex 31:13, emphasis added).

Early Christians recognized the mark of God's authority. In the first one hundred year history of the church, you will find no discussion of the Sabbath question. But over the following three hundred years, there is much debate recorded.

Church history reveals the Roman government first endeavored to erase God's Sabbath commandment. They faced stiff resistance to the conversion of Sabbath worship to Sunday worship among the faithful. The Roman Catholic Papacy knew how to deal with such resistance.

The Council of Laodicea, A.D. 364, passed a law (Canon XXIX) which decreed: "Christians shall not Judaize and be idle on Saturday but shall work on that day; but the Lord's day they shall especially honor, and as being Christians, shall, if possible, do no work on that day. If, however, they are found Judaizing, they shall be shut out from Christ" (Charles J. Hefele, *A History of the Christian Councils,* Vol. 2, page 316).

The issuance of this decree proves two things to me. First, Christians were still worshiping on the Sabbath over three hundred years after Christ's ascension to heaven. That's why the Roman Catholic Church had to take action against them. Second, the Roman Papacy was willing to stamp out those who followed God's recorded instructions, rather than the methods devised by man.

On the strength of this law, historians report that the penalty for worshiping on the Sabbath was *death!* Many were martyred. Many more acquiesced to save their lives. Will history repeat itself?

Who is responsible for introducing the controversy—this Sunday-keeping tradition of man? Working through human agents, Satan positioned himself to destroy the sign of God's authority—the holy Sabbath day of the Lord.

Satan desires to be "like the Most High" (Is 14:14). Ever since he tempted Eve in the garden, the archenemy of our souls has continued to introduce doubt and disbelief in the Word of God to gain a foothold in our lives.

Satan wants to make Sunday the mark of his authority. By manipulating the prescribed day and time of God's commandment, he now has many deceived worshipers of the true God worshiping on a day authorized only by his influence on a religious system—a system that mocks most Protestants. Consider the following correspondence:

Thomaston, Georgia
May 22, 1954

Pope Pius XII, Rome, Italy

Dear Sir:

Is the accusation true, that Protestants accuse you of? They say you changed the Seventh Day Sabbath to the, so-called Christian Sunday: Identical with the First Day of the week. If so, when did you make the change, and by what authority?

Yours very truly,
J. L. Day

The Reply:

THE CATHOLIC EXTENSION MAGAZINE
180 Wabash Ave., Chicago, Illinois
(Under the Blessing of Pope Pius XII)

Dear Sir:

Regarding the change from the observance of the Jewish Sabbath to the Christian Sunday, I wish to draw your attention to the facts:

(1) That Protestants, who accept the Bible as the only rule of faith and religion, should by all means go back to the observance of the Sabbath. The fact that they do not, but on the contrary observe Sunday, stultifies them in the eyes of every thinking man.

(2) We Catholics do not accept the Bible as the only rule of faith. Besides the Bible we have the living Church, as a rule to guide us. We say, this Church instituted by Christ, to teach and guide men through life, has the right to change the Ceremonial laws of the Old Testament and hence, we accept her change of the Sabbath to Sunday. We frankly say, "yes," the Church made this change, made this law, as she made many other laws, for instance, the Friday Abstinence, the unmarried priesthood, the laws concerning mixed marriages, the regulation of Catholic marriages, and a thousand other laws.

(3) We also say that of all Protestants, the Seventh-day Adventists are the only group that reason correctly and are consistent with their teachings. It is always somewhat laughable to see the Protestant Churches, in pulpit and legislature, demand the observance of Sundays of which there is nothing in the Bible.

> With best wishes
> Peter R. Tramer, Editor

If you think about it, isn't it funny that Protestants, who profess to go by the Bible and the Bible only, are demanding Sunday observance and trying to prop up Sunday laws? Catholics find it "laughable," because there is no scriptural support for this staunch stand.

Yet, many Protestants say, "What difference does it make? At least I'm taking a day to worship the Lord!" Others say, "I keep every day holy."

The component missing from their reasoning is that God blessed and sanctified the *day*—not the *rest*. And God's definition of keeping a day *holy* is to cease all secular work (Ex 20: 8-11), refrain from buying and selling (Neh 10:31, 13:15-22), and to focus on Him as our delight, rather than worldly pleasures (Is 58:13-14).

No one can keep every day holy in the eyes of the Lord! More importantly, only God can bless and sanctify a day, declaring it to be sacred to Him—as He did with the Sabbath, calling it "My holy day."

God's ways are higher than our ways. They don't always make sense to us. Do you remember the story of Naaman, the commander of the Syrian armies who was afflicted with leprosy? The narrative is recorded in 2 Kings, chapter five.

When the prophet of the Lord, Elisha, sent word for him to dip seven times in the muddy Jordan River to be healed, Naaman was insulted. Still, his servants convinced him to try God's way.

Dipping once, twice ... six times, surely Naaman felt ridiculous. What if he had stopped at the sixth time? Healing would have eluded him. But on the seventh dip into the Jordan, healing came.

Why? Because God had placed the blessing on the *seventh* time. Can you see the connection to God's blessing on the seventh day?

Did God intend His Sabbath to be a mere religious observance? No! He created it to be a day to celebrate our relationship with Him. The *day* is merely an outward symbol of whom we recognize as the supreme authority over our lives.

This is not a minor issue. In fact, it becomes a life and death issue when the prophetic *mark of the beast* is imposed.

If there's one thing I admire about the Catholic Church, it's the position they so clearly state that Sabbath-breaking is a matter of serious consequence. They rightfully declare Sabbath-breaking to be an *apostasy, a turning away* from God's truths.

Paul would have a word of warning for us, "Beware lest anyone cheat you through philosophy and empty deceit, according to the tradition of men ... and not according to Christ" (Col 2:8). In other words, don't accept a counterfeit.

I want to share a quote I found online. If you have access to the Internet, you can read multiple articles on this topic from the Catholic Church. Their online address is www.immaculateheart.com—when the home page appears, click on "MaryOnLine," and then click "Rome's Challenge."

There's some fascinating reading from this series of articles published in the Church magazine, *The Catholic Mirror.* In case you don't have Internet access, let me share a sampling of what this website contains.

The MaryOnLine+ editors write this—

"... The challenge issued by Rome over 100 years ago remains: Either the Catholic Church is right, or the Seventh Day Adventists are right. There can be no other choice.

"And if one choose neither, then the whole doctrine of Sola Scriptura collapses, and with it, the pillar upon which all of Protestantism stands. What one has left is an invented religion, an invented God, and an invented set of beliefs that suits man's purpose, and not the Creator's.

"Like Satan and Luther before them, Protestants have spoken the creed, in action and in thought, if not in word, 'I Will Not Serve.' The challenge remains—yet, you will find no response, not from any Evangelical, Fundamentalist, or mainline Protestant denomination anywhere. Ultimately, it is the clear authority of the Catholic Church as vested in her by God Himself, that rules the day ... ."

Now, here's another quote from *The Catholic Mirror* that I found at this website. It's a number of paragraphs, but well worth your consideration. The Catholic Church is well versed on the topic of God's holy Sabbath day—

"... The teacher [of the Protestants, the Bible] demands emphatically in every page that the law of the Sabbath be observed every week ... the disciples of that teacher have not once for over three hundred years observed the divine precept! That immense concourse of Biblical Christians, the Methodists, have declared that the Sabbath has never been abrogated. ... God's written word enjoins His worship to be observed on Saturday absolutely, repeatedly, and most emphatically... .

"... Proposing to follow the Bible only as teacher, yet before the world, the sole teacher is ignominiously thrust aside, and the teaching and practice of the Catholic Church—'the mother of abomination,' when it suits their purpose so to designate her—adopted, despite the most terrible threats pronounced by God Himself against those who disobey the command, 'Remember to keep holy the Sabbath.'

"Before closing this series of articles, we beg to call the attention of our readers once more to our caption, introductory of each: 1. The Christian Sabbath, the genuine offspring of the union of the Holy Spirit with the Catholic Church His spouse. 2. The claim of Protestantism to any part therein proved to be groundless, self-contradictory, and suicidal.

"The first proposition needs little proof. The Catholic Church for over one thousand years before the existence of a Protestant, by virtue of her divine mission, changed the day from Saturday to Sunday ... .

"The Protestant world at its birth found the Christian Sabbath too strongly entrenched to run counter to its existence: it was therefore placed under the necessity of acquiescing in the arrangement, thus implying the

Church's right to change the day, for over three hundred years. The Christian Sabbath is therefore to this day, the acknowledged offspring of the Catholic Church as spouse of the Holy Ghost, without a word of remonstrance from the Protestant world.

"Let us now, however, take a glance at our second proposition, with the Bible alone as the teacher and guide in faith and morals. This teacher [the Bible] most emphatically forbids any change in the day for paramount reasons.

"The command calls for a 'perpetual covenant.' The day commanded to be kept by the teacher has never once been kept, *thereby developing an apostasy* from an assumedly fixed principle, as self-contradictory, self-stultifying, and consequently as suicidal as it is within the power of language to express.

"Nor are the limits of demoralization yet reached. Far from it. Their pretense for leaving the bosom of the Catholic Church was for apostasy from the truth as taught in the written word.

"They adopted the written word as their sole teacher, which they had no sooner done than they abandoned it promptly, as these articles have abundantly proved; and by a perversity as willful as erroneous, they accept the teaching of the Catholic Church in direct opposition to the plain, unvaried, and constant teaching of their sole teacher in the most essential doctrine of their religion, thereby emphasizing the situation in what may be aptly designated 'a mockery, a delusion, and a snare.'"

Now that's a bold statement, isn't it? Still, the grave truth of their accusation against Protestants accepting the change to Sunday as "thereby developing an apostasy" is accurate. Sabbath-keeping is about loyalty to God. I must agree with the Catholic Church in this instance—according to the Bible, Sabbath-breaking is an apostasy.

In fact, this is Satan's strategy to cause separation between

God and man. Do you see how Satan is trying to establish his mark of authority by exalting a counterfeit over the true Sabbath of God's Word?

As you continue reading this book, I hope to prove from Scripture that Christians have been beguiled by a doctrine of Beelzebub! And we calmly christen it *a tradition of man*.

In the crisis hour of earth's climax, God's Sabbath becomes critical. It will determine allegiance to either the God of the universe or the prince of the power of darkness.

In His abundant grace, God winked at our ignorance in the past. "Truly, these times of ignorance God overlooked, but now commands all men everywhere to repent, because He has appointed a day on which He will judge the world in righteousness by the Man whom He has ordained ..." (Acts 17:30-31).

The sleeping church needs to be revived to the truth of the Lord's Day! A time of crisis is coming when the mark of authority on our lives will have eternal consequences.

The books of Daniel and Revelation, prophetic warnings of end-time events, are veiled in symbolic language. They speak of a beast power that stands in the place of God, and another apostate group who form an "image" to the beast. Revelation depicts a voice from heaven calling His people out of spiritual Babylon—for the sake of their lives.

Have you ever felt a foreboding frustration in reading those two Bible books? God did not leave the symbolism to private interpretation. He gave us all the answers in Scripture.

In the next chapter, we'll let the Bible interpret the symbols of Daniel and Revelation, unveiling their meaning to lay out God's end-time message in a manner that cannot be doubted or misunderstood.

To conclude this chapter, I couldn't say it any better than this quote from the *Catholic Mirror*, dated December 1893—

"Reason and common sense demand the acceptance of one of the other of these alternatives: either Protestantism and the keeping holy of Saturday, or Catholicity and the keeping holy of Sunday. Compromise is impossible."

9

The "Antichrist Beast"—

Part 1

Are you familiar with *Cliff Notes*™—the educational resource famous for condensing classic books into concise summaries? Desperate students often turn to *Cliff Notes*™ to understand complex reading materials in a hurry. They don't walk away experts, but at least they gain a general understanding of the author's presentation.

Well, this chapter and the next three will be similar in nature. We will review a condensed Bible version of the prophetic *beast* and his *mark*. You won't walk away an expert on end-time events, but I hope you clearly see from Scripture that God did not leave it up to man to make a private interpretation of the figurative language of prophecy.

> **"And so we have the prophetic word confirmed, which you do well to heed as a light that shines in a dark place, until the day dawns ... knowing this first, that no prophecy of Scripture is of any private interpretation"**
> *2 Peter 1:19-20*

The Bible explains itself! All the symbols from the books of Daniel and Revelation are defined somewhere within the

Scriptures. It's time to return to the Bible and wash away the tangled web of man's private opinions.

Who is the "little horn" power of the book of Daniel? Who is the "antichrist" referred to in 1st and 2nd John? What are the "beast" power and the "image" of the beast that Revelation mentions? What is the "mark of the beast" that God warns us not to receive?

So much error has crept into the church since the mid-1900s. Protestants have lost touch with the Bible truths that triggered the Reformation. With the wildly oscillating interpretations of Revelation, some believers have given up on understanding end-time events.

It doesn't have to be that way! A systematic study of the books of Daniel and Revelation will provide all the answers we need. And we desperately need answers. It's critical we understand the approaching unholy alliance that will unleash its fury on Planet Earth.

Different Schools of Prophetic Interpretation

In the sixteenth century, a close study of Scripture and history caused Protestant Reformers to identify the *Roman Papal system* as the antichrist power of prophecy. Reformers also discovered that documents of the early Christian era verified their findings—Christian leaders of the past had made the identical conclusion.

Broadcasting these views, the Reformers put the Papacy in an uproar. To counteract the damage to Papal dominion, Jesuit priests were commissioned to present a new interpretation—an interpretation that would point the finger of prophecy away from the Papacy.

Most Protestants today would be shocked to learn a Catholic priest developed the now popular interpretation of Revelation—including the "rapture and left behind" theory.

I think it will be eye opening for us to review briefly the history of prophetic interpretation. How can we weigh the validity of a viewpoint without knowing its source? It's important to know where teachings originated and how they gained entrance into mainstream Christianity.

There are several schools of prophetic interpretation—historicism, futurism, preterism, and idealism:

- *Historicists* interpret the prophecies of Daniel and Revelation as covering the chain of historical events— beginning at the time the prophet wrote and following the natural sequence of history—to the establishment of God's kingdom on earth. This disciplined method of following history's flow eliminates *private* interpretations.
- *Futurists* create a great gap in the time-line of prophecy, placing most of Daniel and Revelation at the very end of the age (including the prophecies of the antichrist, the beast, and the 1260 days of persecution). They consider the era of the Christian church to be an interim period—a sort of *time out*—with no prophetic fulfillment.
- *Preterists* think most of the events of Revelation already took place in its first-century setting.
- *Idealists* think Revelation is a story of the struggle between good and evil but has no historical reference.

Historicists believe prophecies were given in *visionary circles* that parallel one another. In other words, they recognize each subsequent prophetic vision to *restate* information and *expand* understanding—by either adding new information, or reviewing the vision from a different time perspective. This is what the angel interpreter did in Daniel (chapters 2, 7 and 8), as we will soon review from Scripture.

The *historicist* method of interpretation prevailed up to the fifth century A.D. It was revived during the Protestant Reformation. Historicists identified the Papacy as the little horn power, the antichrist system, and the beast of Revelation.

Championing the early Christian era beliefs, Protestant Reformers created quite a stir against the Roman Catholic Church. To counteract the historicist claims, two Jesuit priests molded new methods of interpretation—preterism and futurism were born.

The *preterist* interpretation, developed by Jesuit priest Luis de Alcazar (1554-1613), identified Nero as the antichrist. He linked the prophecies of Daniel to the time of the Maccabeans, and the events of Revelation to the time of the Apostle John.

The Jesuit priest Francisco Ribera (1537-1591) developed the *futurist* interpretation. He randomly lopped off the final week of the Daniel 9 seventy-week time prophecy, and positioned it as a seven-year period just before Christ's second coming. We will examine this in a moment.

Ribera identified the antichrist as a single person, an evil ruler who is at first welcomed by the Jews and helps to rebuild the temple in Jerusalem. In his explanation, this evil ruler breaks the treaty in the midst of a seven-year period, abolishes Christianity, and rules the world for 42 months of tribulation.

In 1950, a commentary on Revelation republished Ribera's writings. At that time, the prevailing Protestant view still identified the Papacy with the Antichrist. But the *futurist* interpretation of the Jesuit priest was given new life and soon swept through the Protestant sector.

John Nelson Darby, founder of the Plymouth Brethren, supported the doctrines of Dispensationalism. Darby divided world history into seven time periods, and declared that God's justice was dispensed differently to the people of each era. According to his teachings, the Jews would be restored as the people of God to rule the nations—under the Mosaic code—in a millennial kingdom on earth.

Darby's interpretations were influenced immensely by Ribera's writings. In turn, C. I. Scofield developed his commentary from Darby's writings. As *Scofield's Study Notes* and the *Scofield Bible* got a foothold in modern Protestant seminaries, Ribera's influence came crashing like a tidal wave into our generation. Many sincere Christians were swept away by the intrigue of this interpretation.

Have you ever felt frustrated in your attempt to grasp the meaning of Daniel and Revelation? How many different explanations have you heard for the *mark of the beast?* How many personalities have futurists labeled as the possible *antichrist?* The speculation that dominates the futurist school of interpretation varies wildly.

The Apostle John promises a blessing to those who study Revelation, "Blessed *is* he who reads and those who hear the words of this prophecy" (Rev 1:3). But how can the ordinary person make sense of the order of events in Revelation?

Let me share a fascinating side-note with you that will be very helpful. A common mistake people make is to assume Revelation lists events in chronological order.

To gain better understanding of this end-time book of prophecy, we need to appreciate the artistic style in which John recorded it. Revelation was written in a literary style called a *chiasm* (KIE-asm). A chiasm lists related items twice, with the order of their listings being reversed. This gives Revelation a *mirror-like* organization.

Here's how it works. The prologue (1:1-8) mirrors the epilogue (22:8-17)—the message to the seven churches (1:10-3:22) mirrors the message of the New Jerusalem (21:9-22:9)—the message of the seven seals (4:1-8:1) mirrors the Millennium message (19:11-21:8)—and so on throughout the book. It's not our purpose to examine this now, but isn't that an intriguing literary style? Understanding this organization will help you grasp Christ's revelation to John.

For our discussion, we will start in Daniel, the little book of prophecy that was to be sealed "until the time of the end" (Dan 12:4). We can't understand the book of Revelation unless we understand the parallel prophecies of Daniel.

The book of Daniel is the key that unlocks many of the symbols of Revelation. In fact, when John was given this "little book" (Rev 10), he had a bittersweet experience as he began to digest it.

The Beasts (Kingdoms) of Daniel

"Those great beasts ... *are* four kings *which* arise out of the earth" (Dan 7:17).

In Daniel, chapter 2, God gives King Nebuchadnezzar a prophetic dream of the world's future, and the events of the latter days of earth's history. "But there is a God in heaven who reveals secrets, and He has made known to King Nebuchadnezzar what will be in the latter days ..." (Dan 2:28).

In the dream, the King saw a great statue that had four divisions of metal. God gave Daniel the interpretation, explaining the statue represented the order of world kingdoms.

The statue's *head of gold* was Nebuchadnezzar's kingdom of Babylon, "... You *are* this head of gold." (Dan 2:38). This kingdom reigned from 603-538 B.C. As the premier metal *(gold)* represented Babylon, so also did the king of beasts *(lion)* in Daniel 7:4.

The next division was the *chest of silver* on the statute, which represented the Medo-Persian Empire. This kingdom reigned from 538-331 B.C. The *bear* of Daniel 7:5 is another symbol for this empire, and the *two-horned ram* identifies it later, "The ram which you saw, having the two horns—*they are* the kings of Media and Persia" (Dan 8:20).

The statue's *brass thighs* represented Greece, which

reigned over the world from 331-168 B.C. The *leopard with four heads* (Dan 7:6) represented the four generals who divided the Grecian Empire when Alexander the Great died. Another symbol used for Greece was the *one-horned goat*, "And the male goat *is* the kingdom of Greece. The large horn that *is* between its eyes *is* the first king [Alexander]" (Dan 8:21).

The *iron legs* of the statue represented the pagan Roman Empire. "… The fourth beast shall be a fourth kingdom on earth, which shall be different from all *other* kingdoms, and shall devour the whole earth, trample it and break it in pieces" (Dan 7:23). Pagan Rome ruled the world with an iron fist from 168 B.C.—A.D. 476. In Daniel 7:7, it is represented as the beast with the *iron teeth.*

The statue's *feet and ten toes*, partly of iron and partly of clay (Dan 10:33, 42), represented the ten original tribes (monarchies) of Western Europe that were the successors to the pagan Roman Empire. No kingdom ever toppled the Romans. When it crumbled from within, it divided into ten smaller kingdoms—

(1) Anglo-Saxons—*modern day England,* (2) Alemanni—*Germany,* (3) Visigoths—*Spain,* (4) Franks—*France,* (5) Lombards—*Italians,* (6) Burgundians—*Switzerland,* (7) Suevi—*Portugal,* (8) Heruli—*uprooted,* (9) Ostrogoths—*uprooted,* and (10) Vandals—*uprooted.*

The Bible tells us these countries will never come under one single ruler again (Dan 2:43). Too bad Constantine the Great, Napoleon, Kaiser Wilhelm, and Hitler didn't recognize this. Just think of the grief that knowledge could have spared.

	Daniel 2	Daniel 7	Daniel 8
Babylon	Gold Head	Lion	
Medo/Persia	Silver Chest	Bear	Ram
Greece	Brass Thighs	Leopard	Goat
Roman Empire	Iron Legs	Iron-Teethed Beast	
Ten Tribes	Feet	Ten Horns	

The Little Horn Power of Daniel 7

In vision, Daniel saw the fourth beast rise up with huge iron teeth and ten horns (Dan 7:7). This is a parallel vision to the statute's iron legs and feet with ten toes—an example of the visionary circle—restating information and expanding it with more details.

This beast with the iron teeth represented the Roman Empire, the fourth kingdom in the succession of the world powers. The Bible identifies the beast's ten horns as ten kings who arise from the break up of pagan Rome (Dan 7:24)—the ten monarchies we just reviewed.

As Daniel was considering the ten horns of this beast, his attention was suddenly drawn to a *little horn* that he noticed coming up among them. Please carefully consider the identifying marks of the little horn power as we review them:

1. The little horn rises from among the ten horns (nations of Western Europe). "I was considering the horns, and there was another horn, a little one, coming up among them ..." (Dan 7:8).

2. The little horn power arises *after* the other ten monarchies and is *different*. "The ten horns *are* ten kings *who* shall arise from this kingdom. And another shall rise after them; he shall be different from the first *ones*, and shall subdue three kings" (Dan 7:24).

3. The little horn destroys three of the ten monarchies, erasing them from the map. "... Before whom three of the first horns were plucked out by the roots" (Dan 7:8).

4. The little horn power has the eyes of a man *and a boastful mouth*. "And there, in this horn, *were* eyes like the eyes of a man, and a mouth speaking pompous words" (Dan 7:8).

5. The little horn power is greater than the others. "...

114

And the other *horn* which came up, before which three fell, namely, that horn which had eyes and a mouth which spoke pompous words, whose appearance *was* greater than his fellows" (Dan 7:20).

6. The little horn power makes war against God's people. "I was watching; and the same horn was making war against the saints, and prevailing against them ..." (Dan 7:21).

7. The little horn speaks pompously toward God and thinks to alter His times and law. "He shall speak *pompous* words against the Most High, shall persecute the saints of the Most High, and shall intend to change times and law" (Dan 7:25).

8. The little horn power persecutes the saints for 1260 years. "Then *the saints* shall be given into his hand for a time and times and half a time" (Dan 7:25).

Papal Rome (the Roman Catholic Church) is the only power in history that perfectly fits the eight descriptive points of the "little horn power." It rose to power after Imperial Rome divided into the ten nations of Western Europe. It came up from among them.

History records the Papal government stamped out the Vandals (A.D. 454), the Heruli (A.D. 493) and the Ostrogoths (A.D. 538)—wiping them out totally. This explains why no ancestry today can be traced to those bloodlines. After the overthrow of the Ostrogoths, the Papal system grew very strong through the Bishops of Rome.

This little horn power had the "eyes of a man," the Pope—never a *queen*, as was sometimes the case with other nations. It blasphemed God by claiming rights due to God alone, and by mixing paganism with the worship of God.

Because Papal Rome was both a *religious* and a *political* power, it was different from the rest and grew greater than the remaining seven monarchies. A study of the history of the Dark Ages bears witness to the horrors Papal Rome perpetrated against the saints of God. In acts of religious persecution, historians estimate the Papacy—pulling the strings of the puppet-state—put to death between fifty to seventy-five million souls.

Daniel 7:25 declared the little horn power would *think* to change *times and law.* Only one commandment within God's Ten-Commandment Law dealt with the issue of time—the fourth one—"Remember the Sabbath," the seventh day of the week God blessed and claimed as His holy day.

The material presented in chapter seven leaves no doubt who *thought* to change the times of God's law, as this statement also bears witness—

"It was the Catholic Church which ... transferred the rest to the Sunday. ... Thus the observance of Sunday by the Protestants is an homage they pay, in spite of themselves, to the authority of the [Catholic] Church" (Monsignour Louis Segus, *Plain Truth About Protestantism of Today*, p. 213).

Leaders of the early church and the Protestant Reformation understood the Catholic Church to be the *little horn power.* They identified the Papacy as, "MYSTERY, BABYLON THE GREAT, THE MOTHER OF HARLOTS AND OF THE ABOMINATIONS OF THE EARTH" (Rev 17:5).

Protestants who trust the historicist method of interpretation still believe this about the Papacy today.

I want to emphasize something I mentioned in an earlier chapter. God has His people in all churches! Salvation is not secured by the name of the church we attend. Rather, as we submit and commit our lives to Christ, He saves us on an individual basis.

Please don't think I am condemning Christians who attend the Catholic Church. It is not the individual we are examining here, but the *system of religion* that the Bible identifies as counterfeit to God's system.

Time Prophecies of Daniel and Revelation

The time prophecy of Daniel 7:25 is very significant in supporting the historicist interpretation. It explains that the little horn power would persecute the saints for "a time and times and half a time."

Other predictions regarding the reign of this power, and the time-line of its persecutions are: *"a time and times and half a time"* (Rev 12:14), *"forty-two months"* (Rev 13:5), and *"one thousand two hundred and sixty days"* (Rev 12:6).

Do all these descriptions refer to the same event? If so, these time definitions must all be equal. Let's see if a quick review of how time is calculated in prophetic writings will help us determine the truth.

In prophecy, a *time* equaled one year—360 days (the Jewish month was 30 days). *Times* equaled two years—720 days (in Hebrew, a *plural* indicates *two*, unless it has a specific numeral attached to it). *Half a time* equaled half a year—180 days.

A simple addition of 360 plus 720 plus 180, gives us a total of 1260 days. If we divide our total of 1260 days by 30 days in a month, we arrive at 42 months.

So, by doing the math, we can quickly see all these definitions of time are identical in value. *A time and times and half a time* equals *forty-months*—which equals *1260 days.* The time prophecies of Daniel and Revelation reviewed here describe the same time-period.

Time/Times/Half a Time	=	42 Months	=	1260 days
360				
720		42		
180		x 30		
1260 Days	=	1260 Days	=	1260 Days

Prophetic writings are full of figurative language. Most everything is represented in symbols, including time. Since the medieval era, Protestants have interpreted a *symbolic day* to represent a *literal year*. The Bible establishes this *day-for-a-year* principle in Numbers 14:34 and Ezekiel 4:6.

One prophetic day equals one literal year. Therefore 1260 days in prophecy equals 1260 literal years.

Bible prophecy is really an advanced recording of history. Prophecy tells us what will happen in history before it happens. So let's see if the little horn power prevailed over the saints of God for 1260 years.

In A.D. 538, after uprooting the Ostrogoths, the Papacy mushroomed into full power and persecuted God's faithful servants. Moving along the historical date line, if we add 1260 years to that date we arrive at A.D. 1798.

If the time prophecies concerning the Papacy prove accurate, then history must record that pontifical authority was interrupted in 1798. Was there a deadly wound to the little horn power?

Yes, there was. It came at the hand of Napoleon Bonaparte, who was determined to demolish the civil-political power of the Papacy. When Pope Pius VI refused to surrender, Napoleon sent one of his top aides, General Berthier, to Rome to overpower the pope.

On February 10, 1798, Berthier dragged the pope from the altar, ripped his rings from his fingers, and took him captive. He then issued a decree that abolished the civil power of the Roman Catholic Church and established the Papal States as an independent republic—under protection of the French army. The defeated pope died in prison.

"The Papal States, converted into the *Roman Republic,* were declared to be in perpetual alliance with France, but the French general was the real master at Rome ... The territorial possessions of the clergy and monks were declared national property, and their former owners cast into prison.

"The papacy was extinct: not a vestige of its existence remained; and among all the Roman Catholic powers not a finger was stirred in its defence. The Eternal City had no longer prince or pontiff; its bishop was a dying captive in foreign lands; and the decree was already announced that no successor would be allowed in his place." (George Trevor, *Rome: From the Fall of the Western Empire,* p. 440).

Half of Europe thought the Papacy was dead. This deadly wound was inflicted in 1798, just as the Daniel time-prophecy had foretold the history of the little horn power would unfold. But we all know there is more to this story.

In 1929, Mussolini healed the deadly wound by signing the Lateran Treaty, a political agreement which created the Vatican City as an independent nation, and guaranteed sovereignty to the Holy See (the territory ruled by the Pope).

The *San Francisco Chronicle* ran this headline on Tuesday, February 12, 1929: "Mussolini and Gasparri Sign Historic Roman Pact … Heal Wound of Many Years."

In a moment, we'll take a closer look at this mortal wound that was inflicted and then healed. These events were also a direct fulfillment of Bible prophecy about the beast of Revelation 13.

First, let's examine how the *historicist* interpretation of Daniel 9 dramatically differs from the *futurist's* explanation. Remember, *futurists* accept the Jesuit priest Ribera's theory that severs the final seven years from the seventy-week time prophecy and shifts them to the very end of time.

In contrast, this brief overview highlights the *historicist* beliefs of the early church and the Protestant Reformers—

Daniel 9:24—"Seventy weeks are determined for your people and for your holy city, to finish the transgression, to make an end of sins, to make reconciliation for iniquity, to bring in everlasting

righteousness, to seal up vision and prophecy, and to anoint the Most Holy."

Historicists believed the events of Dan 9:24 were fulfilled at Christ's advent. Using the "day-for-a-year" principle, 70 weeks represented 490 literal years.

This time was determined or "cut off" (Hebrew translation) from the 2300-day prophecy of Daniel 8:14. God allotted this period of grace for the Jewish nation to line up with His purposes for calling them as His people.

Christ was anointed as Messiah, the Most Holy. He offered the final atonement for sin at the Cross. He purchased our redemption at Calvary and reconciled us to God.

Daniel 9:25—"Know therefore and understand, that from the going forth of the command to restore and build Jerusalem until Messiah the Prince, there shall be seven weeks and sixty-two weeks; the street shall be built again, and the wall, even in troublesome times."

The decree to rebuild Jerusalem and restore the Jewish nation was issued in 457 B.C. (see Dan 7:25; Ezra 7:11-12). The seven prophetic weeks equaled *49 literal years*.

As prophesied, the rebuilding was completed exactly forty-nine years later in 408 B.C. (see Nehemiah chapters 4-7 to understand the troublous times of their labor).

Now our time calculation gets exciting, because this prophecy foretells the coming of the Messiah. If we take the initial seven prophetic weeks *(49 literal years)* and add the following 62 prophetic weeks *(434 literal years)*, our total is *483 years*.

The book of Daniel proclaimed the Messiah would be announced 483 years from the issuance of the decree to rebuild Jerusalem. What an incredible time prophecy! Let's see if it happened as foretold.

To calculate this date, we must subtract 483 from the year 457 B.C. *(as B.C. dates advance, the year decreases—that's why we subtract).* This calculation gives us 26, but we must take into account the year "zero." To compensate for the "zero" year, we must add one year to our total. This brings us to the year A.D. 27.

According to Daniel 9:24, we should expect the Most Holy to be anointed at the end of this 69-week period, in A.D. 27. Was "Messiah the Prince" revealed on schedule?

Jesus Christ was anointed with the Holy Spirit (Lk 3:22) at His baptism in A.D. 27. As Jesus began His preaching ministry He announced, *"The time is fulfilled,* and the kingdom of God is at hand. Repent, and believe in the gospel" (Mk 1:15).

This amazing time prophecy of Daniel 9:24 convinced Sir Isaac Newton (the famous seventeenth-century physicist, mathematician, and philosopher) that the Bible was the inspired Word of God.

Daniel 9:26-27—"And after the sixty-two weeks Messiah shall be cut off, but not for Himself. … Then he shall confirm a covenant with many for one week; but in the middle of the week He shall bring an end to sacrifice and offering."

These Scriptures depict the 70th week. *After the sixty-two weeks* means the previous period of the *first seven weeks* (rebuilding Jerusalem) must be taken into account. So it represents *after* a total period of 69 prophetic weeks (each week representing seven literal years).

Just as Daniel 9:27 foretold, in the middle of the 70th week (just three and one-half years into His ministry) Jesus was cut off at the Cross and brought sacrifice and offering to an end. His perfect sacrifice, once for all (Heb 10:10), ended the Mosaic law of rituals and ceremonies.

At Christ's direction, His disciples continued confirming the Abrahamic covenant with the Jews for the remaining prophetic half-week. It wasn't until Stephen was stoned, three and a half years later, that Christ called Paul to take the gospel to the Gentiles. The special time for the Jewish nation to *finish their transgressions* had ended.

From Paul's day forward, belonging to the group known as God's *chosen people* would no longer depend on being the *physical descendents* of Abraham.

Who is Israel today? Let's see if Scripture sheds some light on this important issue. The name *Israel* had a spiritual origin. It is a *spiritual* name. When Jacob wrestled all night with God at Peniel, he said, "I will not let You go unless You bless me" (Gen 32:26).

God, in His mercy, more than *allowed* Jacob to prevail— He *empowered* him to prevail. Because Jacob embraced God in faith and refused to be discouraged, the Lord gave him a new *spiritual name,* changing his name to "Israel."

Jacob had lived his life labeled as a "supplanter" (the meaning of Jacob)—one who craftily took the place of another. God changed Jacob's spiritual identity when He labeled him *Israel*—"a prince with God." Afterwards, the descendents of Jacob were called the nation of Israel.

The Apostle Paul wrote, "For they *are* not all Israel who *are* of Israel, nor *are they* all children because they are the seed of Abraham; but, 'In Isaac your seed shall be called'" (Rom 9:6-7). And Paul added, "And if you *are* Christ's, then you are Abraham's seed, and heirs according to the promise" (Gal 3:29).

Today God has a spiritual Israel—a new *chosen* people. The Apostle Peter wrote, "But you *are* a chosen generation, a royal priesthood, a holy nation, His own special people, that you may proclaim the praises of Him who called you out of darkness into His marvelous light; who once *were* not a people but *are* now the people of God, who had not obtained mercy but now have obtained mercy" (1 Pet 2:9-10).

Since the crucifixion of Christ, people of physical Jewish descent become the people of God just as everyone else does— by accepting Jesus Christ as Lord.

To retain the *national* privilege of being God's chosen people and to preserve their holy city, Jerusalem, the nation of Israel was warned they must regain their right standing with God.

God sent His messenger to announce a 70-week period *determined* specifically for the Jews.

But we know they did not respond in the manner God desired. As the middle of the seventieth week closed in on Him, Christ wept over Jerusalem saying, "See! Your house is left to you desolate" (Mt 23:38).

Are we to believe—as the Jesuit Ribera proposed—that when God decreed, "Seventy weeks are determined for your people and for your holy city" that He really meant sixty-nine? In fact, the angel said all the events would happen *within* the seventy prophetic weeks, which were a part of the greater 2300-day prophecy of Daniel 8:14.

How do you remove a week from such a time sequence and still call it the 70th week?

Every rule of logic demands that the 70th week followed the 69th week of Daniel's prophecy. And the evidence of history supports the continuity of this time-line.

Scripture provides no authority to lop it off and place it as the final week before Christ returns. Yet the *futurists* interpret this to mean sixty-nine weeks—plus an interval of two dozen centuries or more before the seventieth week. *Historicists* dismiss this notion as a cleverly devised fable.

Protestant scholars from the sixteenth through early twentieth centuries believed the *historicist* interpretation. Matthew Henry's Bible commentaries are reportedly the most widely used study resources among Protestants of today. Here is an excerpt of his exposition on Daniel 9:26-27—

"The Messiah must be cut off...to atone for our sins, and to purchase life for us ... He must confirm the covenant with many. He shall introduce a new covenant ... He shall confirm by His doctrine and miracles, by His death and resurrection, by the ordinances of baptism and the Lord's supper ...

"He must cause the sacrifice and oblation to cease. By offering Himself a sacrifice once for all He shall put an end to all the Levitical sacrifices, shall supercede them and set them aside; when the substance comes the shadows shall be done away" (*Matthew Henry Unabridged,* Daniel 9:27).

In contrast, the *futurist* interpretation of the Jesuit priest Ribera uses Daniel 9:27 to support the illogical assertion that the temple will be rebuilt in Jerusalem before Christ returns, sacrifices will be restored, the antichrist will confirm a covenant with the Jews, and then he will break it in the middle of the prophetic week.

Aside from the folly of placing the seventieth-week event at the end of time, are we to imagine that God would endorse the restoration of the sacrificial system of the Old Covenant?

Christ sacrificed "once for all." Isn't it more valid to believe that God would consider future animal sacrifices as *trampling* on the blood of Christ?

"Of how much worse punishment, do you suppose, will he be thought worthy who has trampled the Son of God underfoot, counted the blood of the covenant by which he was sanctified a common thing, and insulted the Spirit of grace?" (Heb 10:29).

Remember, the Papacy commissioned Ribera to point the finger of prophecy away from them. His *futuristic* prophetic interpretation—developed entirely by the motivation to deflect attention from the Roman papal system—has permeated the Christian church only since the mid-1900's.

Are you old enough to remember the national concern over electing John F. Kennedy as President of the United States (1961), simply because he was a Catholic? Protestant Americans then still believed the Papacy was the Antichrist.

It wasn't until Ribera's counter-reformation teachings on futurism were republished that Protestants were swayed in another direction—a ploy that played right into the devil's hands to disguise the true antichrist system.

I realize this might be your first introduction to the historicist school of interpretation. I encourage you to spend more time investigating what the leaders of the early church and the Protestant Reformation believed.

If you are new to the study of prophecy, please don't become discouraged if it's difficult to wrap your mind around all of this the first time through. Studying prophecy is much like trying to put a jigsaw puzzle together.

If you have not seen the "picture" on the box that the puzzle originally came in, it's a great challenge to get all the pieces together the first time through. But, once the *big picture* is seen, it's easier to assemble the pieces the second time around.

As we continue over the next few chapters, you will begin to see the *big picture* of prophecy come together. With your field of vision increased, you will find your review of prophecy to be more rewarding each time you try to assemble the symbolic pieces of the prophetic puzzle.

Just remember this—only use the pieces that come in the original box, or you won't have an accurate picture! What do I mean? Well, just as you can't substitute pieces from one jigsaw puzzle for another, you can't substitute man's interpretation for prophetic symbols.

The Bible explains itself! The meaning of each symbol in prophecy is defined somewhere within the Scriptures. God did not leave it up to man to guess the final expression of His will for humanity.

10

The "Antichrist Beast" —

Part 2

Francisco Ribera—the Jesuit priest commissioned by the Papacy to rewrite prophetic interpretation—would surely relish the success of his counter-reformation teaching. It has spread like wildfire, consuming the minds of the Christian majority today.

His idea of a future evil ruler coming as the Antichrist just before Christ returns is now promoted from Protestant pulpits, a popular book series, and movies.

But how could the leaders of the early church and the Reformation logically identify the Papacy as the antichrist system? We'll look at some more evidence in this chapter.

First, we will review what the Bible has to say about the antichrist power.

The Antichrist Power

Many Christians assume the word "antichrist" means *against* Christ. The broader Greek definition is of one who sets himself up "in the place of" Christ.

There are only four Bible references to *antichrist* and one to *antichrists*. Let's see what we can learn from them.

John writes that many antichrists had *already* appeared in his day. He identifies them as coming from *inside* the church—

"Little children ... as you have heard that the Antichrist is coming, even now many antichrists have come, by which we know that it is the last hour. They went out from us ... *they went out* that they might be made manifest, that none of them were of us" (1 Jn 2:18-19).

He also tells us that *antichrist* is anyone who denies the Father and the Son—the ones who try to deceive us with false Christian doctrines—

"Who is a liar but he who denies that Jesus is the Christ? He is antichrist who denies the Father and the Son. These things I have written to you concerning those who *try to* deceive you" (1 Jn 2:22, 26).

In the early Christian church, the antichrist spirit was already working—deceiving people about the nature of Christ, denying that He came in the flesh—

"... Every spirit that does not confess that Jesus Christ has come in the flesh is not of God. And this is the *spirit* of the Antichrist, which you have heard was coming, and is now already in the world" (1 Jn 4:3).

"For many deceivers have gone out into the world who do not confess Jesus Christ *as* coming in the flesh. This is a deceiver and an antichrist" (2 Jn 1:7).

That completes our review of the only Bible Scriptures that use the word *antichrist*. But Peter and Paul also wrote about false church leaders who would arise to teach blasphemous doctrines and lure others from the love of God's truth.

Peter warned of destructive doctrines coming from within the church (2 Pet 2:1-3). And Paul had earlier warned the elders at Ephesus—

"Also from among yourselves men will rise up, speaking perverse things, to draw away the disciples after themselves" (Acts 20:30). Paul also warned Timothy that some would turn away from the truth and follow deceiving spirits, "For the time will come when they will not endure sound doctrine, but according to their own desires …" (2 Tim 4:3).

Followers of Ribera's school of futurism get a lot of mileage out of Paul's reference to the "man of sin." According to futurists, this is the Antichrist who rules the world *after* Christ *secretly* makes His Second Coming. But, in contrast, here's what the Scripture says—

"Let no one deceive you by any means; for *that Day will not come* unless the falling away comes first, and the man of sin is revealed, the son of perdition, who opposes and exalts himself above all that is called God or that is worshiped, so that he sits as God in the temple of God, showing himself that he is God" (2 Thess 2:3-4).

Notice Paul wrote that Christ does not return until *after* the man of sin is revealed. First, there is a falling away from the truth, an apostasy. To exalt the *man of sin* above God, the false system of worship is set up—and revealed. *Then* Christ returns!

Was Paul referring to a single individual or a religious system when he spoke of the *man of sin*? It's helpful to consider that he used a similar, seemingly singular reference to the *man of God*—

"All Scripture *is* given by inspiration of God, and *is* profitable for doctrine, for reproof, for correction, for instruction in righteousness, that the man of God may be complete, thoroughly equipped for every good work" (2 Tim 3:16-17). Did Paul mean to imply that the *man of God* was a single person?

What conclusions can we confidently draw about the antichrist from Scripture?

- There were many antichrists in John's day (1 Jn 2:18).
- These antichrists came from within the church, so they appeared to be Christians (1 Jn 2:19).

- The antichrists taught deceiving doctrines that somehow denied the sovereignty of the Father and the Son (1 Jn 2:22, 26).
- The antichrists deny that Christ was incarnated in man's *flesh nature* (2 Jn 1:7).
- Exalting the *man of sin* above God, they established a false system of worship—setting up someone that usurps the power of God in His church (2 Thess 2:3-4).
- Many fall away from the truth—following after the *man of sin,* who is revealed *before* Christ returns (2 Thess 2:3-4).

In a moment, we'll review some Papal doctrines that will help us understand why the Protestant Reformers identified the Roman Papacy as the little horn power, the *man of sin,* the antichrist, and the beast of Revelation 13.

The Beast of Revelation 13

Now, let's review how Scripture demonstrates that Daniel and Revelation coincide as parallel prophecies. We will see that the little horn power of Daniel—that we studied in chapter nine—is the beast power of Revelation 13.

"Then I stood on the sand of the sea. And I saw a beast rising up out of the sea, having seven heads and ten horns, and on his horns ten crowns, and on his heads a blasphemous name. Now the beast which I saw was like a leopard, his feet were like *the feet of* a bear, and his mouth like the mouth of a lion.

"The dragon gave him his power, his throne, and great authority. And *I saw* one of his heads as if it had been mortally wounded, and his deadly wound was healed. And all the world marveled and followed the beast" (Rev 13:1-3).

This beast of Revelation 13 is a composite symbol. It contains body parts from the four beasts of Daniel 7. It's interesting to note that Revelation mentions the beasts in reverse order from Daniel. Why? The prophetic vision in Daniel was looking forward in history, whereas the Revelation vision given to John looked back over the historic time line.

If we compare this beast of Revelation with the description of the little horn power of Daniel, we see that both make war on God's people (Rev 13:7; Dan 7:21), for the same period of 1260 years, and have a mouth that speaks great things and blasphemies (Rev 13:5; Dan 7:25).

The beast of Revelation 13 rises out of the *sea.* We don't have to guess what the sea symbolized, for the Bible interprets the waters as "peoples, multitudes, nations, and tongues" (Rev 17:15; *see also* Is 17:12-13). It comes up in a populated area of multiple languages.

We discover more detail describing the apparent "mortal wound" and the healing of that wound in Revelation 13:3. "… All the world marveled and followed the beast … and they worshiped the beast, saying, 'Who *is* like the beast? Who is able to make war with him?' … All who dwell on the earth *will* worship him …" (Rev 13:3, 4, 8).

As we studied in the chapter nine segment *Time Prophecies of Daniel and Revelation,* history confirms the Papacy was dealt a deadly wound in 1798 when their civil power was destroyed. It wasn't until 1929, that political authority was restored to the Papacy and the deadly wound was healed.

The Vatican became an independent nation—a power that is not only ecclesiastical, but political. Today, nations around the world recognize her sovereignty by assigning ambassadors to represent them before her king, the Pope. Heads of state—including U.S. Presidents—pay official visits to the Vatican.

Revelation 13 and Daniel 7 are parallel prophecies about the same religio-political power. It's the only world power that meets all the identifying marks. The Bible and world history work together to correctly identify the Papacy as the little horn power, the antichrist, and the leopard-like beast.

But who is the dragon that gives this beast his "power ... throne, and ... authority?" Again, there's no need for guesswork, because Scripture identifies him in the previous chapter—

"So the great dragon was cast out, that serpent of old, called the Devil and Satan, who deceives the whole world ..." (Rev 12:9).

In chapter twelve, we will review Revelation's teachings on the system of spiritual confusion called MYSTERY BABYLON—devised by the great dragon to deceive the whole world (*if possible*), passed down to the Papacy, and imitated by others.

The False System of Worship

Bible prophecies don't condemn *members* of the Roman Catholic Church, or even sincere-hearted priests and leaders who labor under the devil's deception.

In fact, Revelation records the voice from heaven recognizing God's people snared by *spiritual confusion,* calling God's people out of *spiritual Babylon*—

"Come out of her, my people, lest you share in her sins, and lest you receive of her plagues" (Rev 18:4).

However, prophecy does predict the impending doom of the *Papal system*—the one that "opposes and exalts himself above all that is called God or that is worshiped, so that he sits as God in the temple of God, showing himself that he is God" (2 Thess 2:4).

We have already reviewed many reasons why the Papacy was identified as the *little horn power, the antichrist* and *the beast of Revelation 13.* Still, we will address a few more to establish further why the Protestant Reformers and leaders of the early Christian church considered this to be scriptural.

We'll ask the question and let the Papal system of the Catholic Church give us the answer.

Does the Papacy speak pompously, as the little horn power and beast of Revelation 13 did?

The Pope of Rome claims titles that only belong to God. "The Pope is of so great dignity and so exalted that he is not a mere man ... The Pope is as it were God on earth, Sole Sovereign of the faithful of Christ, Chief of Kings, having plenitude of power to whom has been entrusted by the omnipotent God direction not only of the earthly but also, of the heavenly kingdom." (Lucius Ferraris, *Papa II*, Prompta Bibliotheca, Vol. VI, pp. 25, 29).

Here's another example, "... The Pope is not only the representative of Jesus Christ, but he is Jesus Christ Himself, hidden under the veil of flesh" (*The Catholic Standard,* July 1895). Other pompous titles paying homage to the Pope include: "Lord God the Pope," "Holy Father," "Head of the Church," and "Ruler of the World."

Is blasphemy a characteristic of the Papal system, as with the antichrist beast?

"The priest holds the place of the Saviour himself, when ... he absolves from sin. This great power, which Jesus Christ has received from his eternal Father, he has communicated to his priests ... .

"The Jews justly said: *Who can forgive sins but God alone?* But what only God can do by his omnipotence, the priest can also do by saying "Ego te absolvo a peccatis tuis" ["I absolve you from your sins"] ..." (Alphonsus de Liguori, *Dignity and Duties of the Priest; or, Selva,* Brooklyn: Redemptorist Fathers, 1927, pp. 34, 35).

Blasphemy, according to the Bible, is a mortal man claiming a characteristic of God or prerogative of His power. When Jesus said to the paralytic, "Son, your sins are forgiven you," He was accused of speaking blasphemy by those who didn't recognize He was God (Mk 2:5, 7). Forgiveness of sins is the privilege of God alone!

The Bible asserts that there is only One mediator between God and humanity—Jesus Christ! (See 1 Tim 2:5; Jn 14:6; Heb 10:19-22). Priests are standing in the place of God when they claim to absolve sins from their confessional booths.

The doctrine of praying through Mary or other "saints" also thrusts another mediator between God and mankind—in direct defiance of Scripture. This abomination abrogates the worship of Christ as our High Priest mediator—

"Therefore He is also able to save to the uttermost those who come to God through Him, since He always lives to make intercession for them. For such a High Priest was fitting for us, *who is* holy, harmless, undefiled, separate from sinners, and has become higher than the heavens; who does not need daily, as those high priests, to offer up sacrifices, first for His own sins and then for the people's, for this He did once for all when He offered up Himself" (Heb 7:25-27).

The Catholic dogma of *transubstantiation* is another source of blasphemy. This is when, in the Eucharist (communion), the priest claims to turn the bread and wine into the actual body and blood of Jesus Christ. This is what the Papal system has to say about it—

"Thus the priest may, in a certain manner, be called the creator of his Creator, since by saying the words of consecration, he creates, as it were, Jesus in the sacrament, by giving him a sacramental existence, and produces him as a victim to be offered to the eternal Father ... .

"'The power of the priest,' says St. Bernardine of Sienna, 'is the power of the divine person; for the transubstantiation of the bread requires as much power as the creation of the world.' ... 'Let the priest,' says St. Laurence Justinian, 'approach the altar as another Christ.' According to St. Cyprian, a priest at the altar performs the office of Christ ..." (Alphonsus de Liguori, *Dignity and Duties of the Priest; or, Selva,* Brooklyn: Redemptorist Fathers, 1927, pp. 32, 33, 34).

Not only does the Papacy proclaim the priest to be "the creator of his Creator," they ignore the Bible teaching that Christ's sacrifice was "once for all." The Bible clearly states Christ does not need to make another sacrifice (Heb 7:27, 10:10).

When Jesus taught that we must eat His *flesh* and drink His *blood* to abide in Him (Jn 6:56), He later explained these were spiritual words with symbolic meaning (Jn 6:63). In all of the Bible's teachings on the communion bread and fruit of the vine, it is clear within the context that this is a symbolic sacrament.

Does the Papal system—like the antichrist—deny that Jesus came in the flesh?

The doctrine of Immaculate Conception attributes sinlessness to Mary. All of humanity is born with a sin nature. If Mary had no sin nature, then Jesus could not have come in the flesh.

A careful study of Scripture proves that Christ was incarnated with the nature of man, yet remained sinless. (See summary points of the New Covenant, chapter four, for a review.) He more than nailed our sins to the cross. He nailed our old *sin nature* to the Cross!

"The sinlessness of the Virgin Mary and the personal infallibility of the Pope are the characteristic dogmas of modern Romanism, the two test dogmas which must decide the ultimate fate of this system. Both rest on pious fiction and fraud; both present a refined idolatry by clothing a pure humble woman and a mortal sinful man with divine attributes.

"The dogma of the Immaculate Conception, which

exempts the Virgin Mary from sin and guilt, perverts Christianism into Marianism; the dogma of Infallibility, which excepts the Bishop of Rome from error, resolves Catholicism into Papalism, or the Church into the Pope. The worship of a woman is virtually substituted for the worship of Christ, and a man-god in Rome for the God-Man in heaven" (Philip Schaff, *The Creeds of Christendom,* New York: Harper, 1919, Vol. 2, p. 164).

Did the Papacy think to change the times and law of God?

The Papacy not only changed the seventh-day Sabbath—the *time* of God's Law—but also, without remorse, they shed the second commandment.

"You shall not make for yourself a carved image, or any likeness *of anything* that *is* in heaven above, or that *is* in the earth beneath, or that *is* in the water under the earth; you shall not bow down to them nor serve them. For I, the LORD your God, *am* a jealous God ..." (Ex 20:4-5).

To keep the perfect number of the Ten Commandments, the Papacy divides the tenth commandment (on coveting) and makes it commandments nine and ten.

Has the Papacy introduced other destructive doctrines according to their own desires?

One of the Papal dogmas Martin Luther most opposed was the sale of *indulgences,* in order for Catholics—living or dead—to be reconciled to God. The Protestant Waldenses particularly protested the pagan doctrine of purgatory adopted by the Catholic Church.

This is a sampling of teachings that constitute the *false system of worship* created by the Papal system—and sustained by the Roman Catholic Church.

In view of all that we've studied here, can you see why so many Bible scholars have identified the Papal system as the "antichrist" beast of the Bible? In chapter twelve, I think you will understand even more clearly as we identify *the mark of the beast*.

First we must learn what the Bible says about the timing of the Second Coming of Christ. Does Christ return before the *mark of the beast* is imposed upon humanity? Or does Christ return *after* the mark?

The answer is critical—and the Bible is clear. It's time for some "straight talk" from the Scriptures about Christ's Second Coming.

11

Christ Returns
After the Mark

*T*hose who foster the Jesuit Ribera's *futurist* interpretation have so clouded the clear teachings of Scripture, that the majority of Christians today believe in the theory of a rapture *before* the "mark of the beast" is imposed.

The *antichrist agenda* has alarmingly bamboozled these sincere Christian believers. My prayer is to present to you sufficient Scripture references to prove this popular interpretation is a perilous counterfeit.

It's critical to understand how Scripture outlines the events of Christ's Second Coming. The reason the religious majority missed Christ's First Advent is because they wrongly interpreted how He would appear.

Although the Jewish nation eagerly anticipated Messiah's arrival, they thought He would arrive as a conquering King, not as the Lamb of God who would sacrifice His life for their sins. If we misinterpret the manner of His Second Advent, we will misinterpret the *mark of the beast.*

"… Then *I saw* the souls of those who had been beheaded for their witness to Jesus and for the word of God, who had not worshiped the beast or his image, and had not received *his* mark on their foreheads or on their hands. And they lived and reigned with Christ for a thousand years" (Rev 20:4).

It's clear the *mark* is received before the millennial reign of the saints with Christ. The question is: When does the thousand years begin? Does Christ return secretly a second time—then again, for a third time, at the end of a seven-year tribulation?

Does God offer yet another chance to sinners *after* Christ's Second Coming? Before we examine the mark of the beast in the next chapter, let's shed the light of Scripture on His return and the resurrection of the righteous.

The Second Coming of Christ

Have you ever contemplated the experience of being alive at Christ's Second Coming?

It thrills me to think about it! As we review what Scripture shares about His sensational return to earth, I encourage you to imagine yourself among those who witness it first-hand.

1. **Christ is Coming a Second Time!**
   "Christ also, having been offered once to bear the sins of many, will appear a second time for salvation without *reference to* sin, to those who eagerly await Him." *Heb 9:28*
2. **No one Knows the Time of His Coming.**
   "But of that day and hour no one knows, not even the angels of heaven, but My Father only. But as the days of Noah were, so also will the coming of the Son of Man be. For as in the days before the flood, they were eating and drinking, marrying and giving in marriage, until the day that Noah entered the ark, and did not know until the flood came and took them all away, so also will the coming of the Son of Man be." *Mt 24:36-39*

3. **Still, the Time of His Return is Expected by the Righteous.**

"For you yourselves know perfectly that the day of the Lord so comes as a thief in the night. For when they say, 'Peace and safety!' then sudden destruction comes upon them, as labor pains upon a pregnant woman. And they shall not escape. But you, brethren, are not in darkness, so that this Day should overtake you as a thief." *1 Thess 5:2-4*

4. **Deceivers Will Come First, Falsely Claiming to be (or to Represent) Christ.**

Jesus warned, "Take heed that no one deceives you. For many will come in My name, saying, 'I am *He,*' and will deceive many. ... Then if anyone says to you, 'Look, here *is* the Christ!' or, 'Look, *He is* there!' do not believe it. For false christs and false prophets will rise and show signs and wonders to deceive, if possible, even the elect. But take heed; see, I have told you all things beforehand." *Mk 13:5-6, 21-23*

5. **Christ Comes with a Loud Shout—as Commander of All Angels—with a Trumpet Blast.**

"For the Lord Himself will descend from heaven with a shout, with the voice of *the* archangel and with the trumpet of God. ..." *1 Thess 4:16*

6. **His Glorious Appearing Will Flash Across the Skies. Every Eye Will See Him. Some Tremble with Fear—Some with Excitement.**

"For as the lightning comes from the east and flashes to the west, so also will the coming of the Son of Man be." *Mt 24:27* "Behold, He is coming with clouds, and every eye will see Him ... All the tribes of the earth will mourn because of Him. ..." *Rev 1:7*

"Men's hearts failing them from fear and the expectation of those things which are coming on the earth, for the powers of heaven will be shaken. Then they will see the Son of Man coming in a cloud with power and great glory. Now when these things begin to happen, look up and lift up your heads, because your redemption draws near." *Lk 21:26-28*

7. **Christ Returns with His Holy Angels, Ready to Render His Rewards.**

    "For the Son of Man will come in the glory of His Father with His angels, and then He will reward each according to his works." *Mt 16:27* "And behold, I am coming quickly, and My reward *is* with Me, to give to every one according to his work." Rev 22:12

8. **All Who are in Their Graves Will Hear His Voice. He Sends His Angels to Gather Those Who Belong to Him.**

    "Do not marvel at this; for the hour is coming in which all who are in the graves will hear His voice and come forth—those who have done good, to the resurrection of life, and those who have done evil, to the resurrection of condemnation." *Jn 5:28-29* "And He will send His angels with a great sound of a trumpet, and they will gather together His elect from the four winds, from one end of heaven to the other." *Mt 24:31*

9. **The Dead in Christ Rise First—the Righteous Living Are Caught Up with the Clouds of Angels to Meet Christ in the Air.**

    "... And the dead in Christ will rise first. Then we who are alive *and* remain shall be caught up together with them in the clouds to meet the Lord in the air." *1 Thess 4:16-17*

    "... You will be blessed ... for you will be repaid at

the resurrection of the righteous." *Lk 14:14 NASB*

"… This *is* the first resurrection. Blessed and holy *is* he who has part in the first resurrection. Over such the second death has no power, but they shall be priests of God and of Christ, and shall reign with Him a thousand years." *Rev 20:5-6*

10. Christ Crowns the Righteous.

"Blessed *is* the man who endures temptation; for when he has been approved, he will receive the crown of life which the Lord has promised to those who love Him." *Ja 1:12*

"I have fought the good fight, I have finished the race, I have kept the faith. Finally, there is laid up for me the crown of righteousness, which the Lord, the righteous Judge, will give to me on that Day, and not to me only but also to all who have loved His appearing." *2 Tim 4:7-8* "… When the Chief Shepherd appears, you will receive the crown of glory that does not fade away." *1 Pet 5:4*

11. There is No Second Chance for the Wicked.

"When once the Master of the house has risen up and shut the door, and you begin to stand outside and knock at the door, saying, 'Lord, Lord, open for us,' and He will answer and say to you, 'I do not know you, where you are from,' then you will begin to say, 'We ate and drank in Your presence, and You taught in our streets.' But He will say, 'I tell you I do not know you, where you are from. Depart from Me, all you workers of iniquity.'" *Lk 13:25-27*

"Then two *men* will be in the field: one will be taken and the other left. Two *women will be* grinding at the mill: one will be taken and the other left. Watch therefore, for you do not know what hour your Lord is coming." *Mt 24:40-42*

12. In Flaming Fire, Christ Takes Vengeance on the Disobedient.

"… When the Lord Jesus is revealed from heaven with His mighty angels, in flaming fire taking vengeance on those who do not know God, and on those who do not obey … ." *2 Thess 1:7-8* "… The Lord will consume with the breath of His mouth and destroy with the brightness of His coming." *2 Thess 2:8*

Is there anything in Scripture that supports the theory that Christ's Second Coming is a *secret?* The radiance of a single angel in scriptural reports caused men to tremble in fear.

When the skies recede as a scroll and He circles the globe at lightning speed, with ten thousands upon ten thousands of His holy angels, will some not notice His appearance? Every eye will see Him!

And when He shouts with the voice of the Archangel, accompanied by trumpet blasts, are we to think some might sleep through this spectacular event? Earth's residents will either run in fear—trying to hide from His face—or they will look upon their Redeemer in joyful anticipation of His reward.

Great rejoicing will be among the faithful as they witness the resurrection of the righteous. I can imagine a great *hallelujah chorus* coming forth as together they are caught up in the air.

I know it is difficult—sometimes even painful—to *unlearn* a principle we have come to believe. There is so much convincing evidence I would like to share with you that I cannot, because of the condensed nature of this book.

But it might be helpful to review another end-time event before we go on to identify the mark of the beast.

The Resurrection of the Righteous

The Bible clearly speaks of only two *universal* resurrections—the resurrection of life and the resurrection of condemnation. Let me give you a brief summary in my own words, and then I'll list the supporting Scriptures.

The resurrection of the righteous takes place at the beginning of the thousand years. As we have already studied, they receive their reward when they wake from their graves. The Bible explains they put on "immortality" at this first resurrection, and have no part in the *second death.*

- "… This *is* the first resurrection. Blessed and holy *is* he who has part in the first resurrection. Over such the second death has no power, but they shall be priests of God and of Christ, and shall reign with Him a thousand years" (Rev 20:5-6).
- Jesus said, "Do not marvel at this; for the hour is coming in which all who are in the graves will hear His voice and come forth—those who have done good, to the resurrection of life, and those who have done evil, to the resurrection of condemnation" (Jn 5:28-29).
- "And many of those who sleep in the dust of the earth shall awake, some to everlasting life, some to shame *and* everlasting contempt" (Dan 12:2).
- "I have hope in God, which they themselves also accept, that there will be a resurrection of *the* dead, both of *the* just and *the* unjust" (Acts 24:15).
- "And you will be blessed … for you shall be repaid at the resurrection of the just" (Lk 14:14).
- "For as in Adam all die, even so in Christ all shall be made alive. But each one in his own order: Christ the firstfruits, afterward those *who are* Christ's *at His coming* … (1 Cor 15:22-23).

- "In a moment, in the twinkling of an eye, at the last trumpet. For the trumpet will sound, and the dead will be raised incorruptible, and we shall be changed. For this corruptible must put on incorruption, and this mortal *must* put on immortality. So when this corruptible has put on incorruption, and this mortal has put on immortality, then shall be brought to pass the saying that is written: 'Death is swallowed up in victory'" (1 Cor 15:52-54).

The Resurrection of the Condemned

The resurrection of the condemned happens at the end of the thousand years. They are raised for the execution of final judgment, and then thrown into the *lake of fire*—to experience the *second death*.

- "But the rest of the dead did not live again until the thousand years were finished" (Rev 20:5). *In modern writing, this quote would be offset by parenthesis (as the New International Version has done). The original Bible transcripts didn't include punctuation, or chapter and verse distinctions. To understand the text here, you must take verses 4-6 as a single reading.*
- "And I saw the dead, small and great, standing before God, and books were opened. And another book was opened, which is *the Book* of Life. And the dead were judged according to their works, by the things which were written in the books. The sea gave up the dead who were in it, and Death and Hades delivered up the dead who were in them. And they were judged, each one according to his works. Then Death and Hades were cast into the lake of fire. This is the second death" (Rev 20:12-14).

- "And anyone not found written in the Book of Life was cast into the lake of fire. ... The cowardly, unbelieving, abominable, murderers, sexually immoral, sorcerers, idolaters, and all liars shall have their part in the lake which burns with fire and brimstone, which is the second death" (Rev 20:15, 21:8).

- "'For behold, the day is coming, burning like an oven, and all the proud, yes, all who do wickedly will be stubble. And the day which is coming shall burn them up ... that will leave them neither root nor branch. ... You shall trample the wicked, for they shall be ashes under the soles of your feet on the day that I do *this*,' Says the LORD of hosts" (Mal 4:1, 3).

If God is love, how can He destroy the wicked in such a manner? The Bible tells us that His infinite love is not willing that *any* should perish (2 Pet 3:9). Still, He created man as a free moral agent—one who has choices.

God will not force anyone to accept His self-sacrificing love. But listen to His heart—"I thought you would call Me my Father and would not turn away from following Me" (Jer 3:19 Amp).

The wicked destroy themselves. By evil choices or by apathy, they reject God's pardoning love and power over sin. The Lord said—

"Have you not brought this on yourself, in that you have forsaken the LORD your God When He led you in the way?...Your own wickedness will correct you, and your backslidings will rebuke you. Know therefore and see that *it is* an evil and bitter *thing* that you have forsaken the LORD your God, and the fear of Me *is* not in you" (Jer 2:17, 19).

The Light of His Countenance will consume evil like a flaming fire. Unholy beings cannot stand in His Presence. Those who are saved will be eternally grateful that everlasting life was a gift from God. We should always be mindful that He is the One Who sanctifies us, making us holy.

As for those who have yet to receive His gift of eternal life, this is what God says to them now—

"Cast away from you all the transgressions which you have committed, and get yourselves a new heart and a new spirit. For why should you die ... ? For I have no pleasure in the death of one who dies ... Therefore turn and live!" (Ezek 18:31-32).

Toward the end of time, God sends three angelic messengers to warn the inhabitants of earth to return to Him. The urgency of their message will turn God's people back to true worship and call them out of *spiritual Babylon.* We will look at those special messages in the next chapter, because they will help us understand the *mark of the beast.*

If we dismiss Jesuit Ribera's *futurist* interpretation (lopping off the final week of Daniel's time prophecy) and hold to the teachings of the early church and the Protestant Reformers, we can also dismiss the idea of the *secret rapture* and the popular *left behind theory.*

And we can dismiss the idea that the *mark of the beast* is not imposed before Christ returns—

> **"Then I saw the souls of those who had been beheaded for their witness to Jesus and for the word of God, who had not worshiped the beast or his image, and had not received his mark on their foreheads or on their hands. And they lived and reigned with Christ for a thousand years."** *Revelation 20:4*

The Scriptures we have just reviewed clearly prove that the *mark of the beast* will be imposed before Christ returns—before He resurrects the righteous—before His angels gather His elect to meet Him in the air—before we spend a thousand years in heaven with Him.

I hope the Bible study of these last three chapters proved the fallacy of Ribera's argument and revealed it as an evil stroke of genius to point the finger away from the Papacy. The prophetic interpretation composed by the Jesuit Ribera was nothing less than Lucifer's lullaby, trying to allure our attention away from his antichrist agenda.

If we aren't aware of this delusion, it could lull the faithful into a sleepy acceptance of the *mark of the beast.*

12

Mark of the Beast

*I*n this chapter, we will unveil the truth of end-time events that lead to the *mark of the beast.* We will also look to Scripture to identify this morbid *mark* and determine how it will be enforced.

Who is the persecuting power that promotes this mark to be received in the *forehead* or in the *hand?* Is this a literal branding of humanity? An implanted computer chip or other device, as some have suggested?

Or—could it be that the symbolic language of prophetic Scripture warns of something altogether different than the popular theories touted today?

Before we begin, let's refresh our memories with a review of several points our study of prophecy has revealed so far—

- The Bible interprets itself—there can be no *private* interpretation (2 Pet 1:19).
- We must look to Scripture to identify prophetic symbols. For example: a "beast" in prophecy is a *kingdom* or *nation* (Dan 7:23)—"sea" or "waters" represents a multitude of people (Rev 17:15; Is 17:12-13).
- In prophetic language, a "day" equals a *literal year* (Num 14:34; Ez 4:6).

- Prophecy is really history written in advance—world history should prove Bible prophecies.
- The literal Greek translation of *antichrist* means one who set himself up *in the place of* Christ.
- Leaders of the early church and the Protestant Reformation identified the Papacy as the antichrist power of 1st and 2nd John, the little horn power of Daniel 7, and the beast of Revelation 13.
- The Jesuit priest Franciso Ribera changed the time-line of Daniel 9:24-27—lopping off the seventieth week and placing it at the end of time—to point the prophetic finger away from the Papacy.
- Before Christ returns, there will be an apostasy—a falling away from the truth into a false system of worship—and the *man of sin* who exalts the false system of worship will be revealed (2 Thess 2:3-4).
- The Second Coming of Christ will not be a secret event (see chapter 11).
- Christ returns *after* the mark of the beast has been imposed on humanity (Rev 20:4).

The *antichrist beast power*—identified as the Roman Papal system of the Vatican nation—is *not* the nation that will enforce the *mark of the beast.* This Bible fact surprises many uninformed Christians.

Revelation depicts a second beast—a different nation—that rises to the occasion. This government power will create an apostate system of worship that is an *image* of the first beast (Roman Catholicism).

We will soon see that, at the time of the end, this second beast-nation causes all of humanity to receive a *mark,* or else suffer great trials and tribulations.

Don't you think it's important for us to recognize the identity of this ominous beast?

Let's search the Scriptures and see if we can logically identify it.

The Second Beast of Revelation 13

"Then I saw another beast coming up out of the earth, and he had two horns like a lamb and spoke like a dragon. And he exercises all the authority of the first beast in his presence, and causes the earth and those who dwell in it to worship the first beast, whose deadly wound was healed." *Rev 13:11-12*

The second beast rises with these identifying prophetic marks: It comes up from the earth; the time it rises is around the time of the wounding of the "first beast" (1798); it is lamblike and has two horns; and it speaks like a dragon. Let's decipher the prophetic code.

In contrast to coming from the sea (which symbolized a densely populated area), this nation comes forth from the *earth*—representing an opposite symbolic meaning (a sparsely populated area). Revelation 12:16 also described the *earth* as a place that was a refuge for the *woman* (church) when the *dragon* (Satan) was persecuting her.

In Revelation, the symbol of a *lamb* represented Christ (Rev 5:12). *Horns* in Bible language are a metaphor to depict powers (Ps 18:2; Lk 1:69).

So far we know this nation would arise around 1798, from a sparsely populated area that was a refuge to persecuted Christians, and would appear to be a peaceable Christian nation (lamblike), with a government based on separation of powers (two-horned).

Surprisingly, the text we are reviewing prophesies this same nation will eventually become a persecuting power that speaks like a dragon (vs. 11).

According to the Bible, the first beast power (Roman

Papacy) and this second beast-nation of Revelation 13 will eventually harmonize to persecute and oppress God's people. The lamblike nation exercises all the authority of the first power and "causes the earth and those who dwell in it to worship the first beast, whose deadly wound was healed" (vs. 12).

> **"And he [the second beast] deceives those who dwell on the earth ... telling [them] to make an image to the beast who was wounded by the sword and lived. He was granted *power* to give breath to the image of the beast ... and cause as many as would not worship the image of the beast to be killed." *Rev 13:14, 15***

This dominating nation deceives the people and causes them to worship the *image* of the first beast (vs. 14), which we have identified as the Roman Papal system. Because of its great power, the lamblike nation breathes life into this false system of worship—creating an existence of authority to be exercised over all.

This seemingly Christian nation threatens anyone who refuses to worship the *image* of the beast with the penalty of death (vs. 15). The persecuting power of the lamblike government comes to the forefront.

> **"He [the second beast] causes all, both small and great, rich and poor, free and slave, to receive a mark on their right hand or on their foreheads, and that no one may buy or sell except one who has the mark or the name of the beast, or the number of his name." *Rev 13:16-17.***

The second beast-nation is the one who has the political power to influence the whole world. This government enforces the *mark of the beast.*

Have the prophetic symbols of Revelation 13 helped you identify this powerful nation?

I thank God that I was born in America—I love my country! Although it saddens me, I must agree with the historicists of today who recognize the lamblike beast of Revelation 13 to be the United States. History and Scripture work together to reveal that the U.S.A. is the only nation that perfectly fits the description of these identifying marks.

The Bible warns us that in a critical hour of history, the U.S. will seek a solution for world crisis. We will study this more in a moment and learn that our government will be deceived. They will think they are doing God a service.

Our Christian-like nation will breathe murderous threats of economic boycott or death to those who won't receive the *mark of the beast* and *worship his image.*

And the faith and patience of the saints will be severely tested.

In advance of this fearful time in history, God graciously sends three angels to warn the inhabitants of the earth. Before we examine the *mark of the beast*, let's take a quick look at God's warning.

The Three Angels' Messages

God broadcasts His end-time message to all who dwell on the earth before the image of the beast emerges—

> **"Then I saw another angel flying in the midst of heaven, having the everlasting gospel to preach to those who dwell on the earth—to every nation, tribe, tongue, and people—saying with a loud voice, 'Fear God and give glory to Him, for the hour of His judgment has come; and worship Him who made heaven and earth, the sea and springs of water.'"** *Rev 14:6-7*

God sends the first of three angels to warn us that the great conflict of earth's final crisis will be over *worship*. Those living just before Christ's return will face a choice—worship the beast and his image, or worship God as Creator of "heaven and earth, the sea and springs of water." *Obedience is the highest expression of worship!*

This prophecy warns us history will repeat itself. Are you familiar with the Daniel 3 account of three Hebrews (Shadrach, Meshach, and Abed-Nego) enslaved by Babylon? This is an example of how the enforcement of false worship promotes persecution.

In ancient Babylon, King Nebuchadnezzar purposely defied God to prove his kingdom would last forever, in spite of God's word to the contrary. The king set up an image of gold and decreed that all must fall down and worship it to pledge their loyalty to his government.

Disobedience to the decree carried the penalty of death. Still, the three Hebrew worthies refused to worship falsely. At the king's command, they were thrown into the furnace. But Christ walked them through their fiery trial and proved to be their salvation.

History will repeat itself.

"And another angel followed, saying, 'Babylon is fallen, is fallen, that great city, because she has made all nations drink of the wine of the wrath of her fornication.'" *Rev 14:8*

The second angel's message from God refers to *spiritual* Babylon. Babylon meant "gate of the gods" and was associated with a Hebrew word meaning *confusion*. This great harlot, *"Mystery Babylon,"* causes the inhabitants of the earth to be drunk with the wine of her false doctrines (Rev 17:2).

The defiance of ancient Babylon is repeated in the end-time *spiritual* Babylon, which creates an atmosphere of false worship, clouded by confusion. The church is to be married to Christ. Spiritual Babylon creates widespread apostasy, causing the church to commit infidelity to the Lord.

> **"Then a third angel followed them, saying with a loud voice, 'If anyone worships the beast and his image, and receives *his* mark on his forehead or on his hand, he himself shall also drink of the wine of the wrath of God, which is poured out full strength into the cup of His indignation. He shall be tormented with fire and brimstone in the presence of the holy angels and in the presence of the Lamb ...'" (Rev 14:9-10).**

Those who accept the mark forfeit eternal life. Their destiny will be to suffer the *second death* in the lake of fire—"the lake that burns with fire and brimstone, which is the second death" (Rev 21:8). But God's faithful will praise the Lord for His promise, "He who overcomes shall not be hurt by the second death" (Rev 2:11).

Before we identify the mark, let me remind you that the Bible must interpret itself. God did not warn us of a mark carrying such eternal consequence without identifying it in Scripture. Although veiled in symbolic language to preserve the writing from being destroyed by its enemies, the Revelation of Christ to His people is complete.

In preparation of these final climatic events, God sends His angels to seal His servants in their foreheads (Rev 7:3). The inhabitants of earth will face a choice that seals their eternal destiny—either they choose to receive the seal of God, or they choose to receive the mark of the beast.

The Seal of God or the Mark of the Beast

God will place His seal in the foreheads of His people.

This seal will be the exact opposite of the mark of the beast. The first question we must answer is, in the symbolic language of Revelation, what does the *forehead* represent? Let's look to Scripture to understand this.

God told shameless Israel, "You have had a harlot's forehead; you refuse to be ashamed" (Jer 3:3). A harlot's *mind* knows no shame.

To Ezekiel God said, "Like adamant stone, harder than flint, I have made your forehead; do not be afraid of them, nor be dismayed at their looks …" (Ez 3:9). God equipped Ezekiel with the courage and character he needed. Making his forehead "harder than flint" meant to make his *mind* strong and unswerving.

Forehead is symbolic language in Scripture for *mind.* God will put some special truth into the *minds* of His people—something that will *mark* them as His. What was God's promise of the New Covenant?

"This *is* the covenant that I will make with them after those days, says the LORD: I will put My laws into their hearts, and in their minds I will write them" (Heb 10:16).

The Ten Commandment Law written on hearts and minds is what identifies God's end-time people. The fourth commandment has the special distinction of carrying the *seal* of God—His name, title and dominion—

"Remember the Sabbath day, to keep it holy … the seventh day *is* the Sabbath of the LORD your God. … For *in* six days the LORD made the heavens and the earth, the sea, and all that *is* in them, and rested the seventh day. Therefore the LORD blessed the Sabbath day and hallowed it" (Ex 20:8-11).

The Sabbath is God's *mark of authority* as Creator God. That explains the first angel's message: "Fear God and give glory to Him, for the hour of His judgment has come; and worship Him who made heaven and earth, the sea and springs of water" (Rev 14:7). Do you recognize the Sabbath commandment language in this message?

Just as Abraham received the *sign* of circumcision as a *seal* of righteousness by faith (Rom 4:11), God's people will receive the *sign* of the Sabbath as a *seal* of our righteousness by faith. "Surely My Sabbaths you shall keep, for it *is* a sign between Me and you … that *you* may know that I *am* the LORD who sanctifies you" (Ex 31:13).

In the closing trials of earth's history, all those who have been "sealed for the day of redemption" by the Holy Spirit (Eph 4:30) will worship in *spirit* and in *truth*—keeping all of God's Ten Commandments.

I want to clarify one point here. What will happen to all of those sincere saints who passed on before, who weren't keeping all of God's commandments?

If they didn't have a chance to learn the truth about the Ten Commandment Law, God will accept them based on their faithfulness to the truths they understood. In heaven, many will celebrate God's Sabbath day for the first time.

But for the generation living just before Christ returns, it will be a different matter. God is shining His light into the darkness even now, and multitudes of people are returning to His seventh-day Sabbath as they learn this truth.

"The path of the just … shines ever brighter unto the perfect day" (Prov 4:18). God *will* get His message to the world before law mandates worship to the image of the beast. With a loud voice, the third angel's message swells to be heard and heeded by the faithful—

"If anyone worships the beast and his image, and receives his mark on his forehead or on his hand, he himself shall also drink of the wine of the wrath of God … ." *Revelation 14:9-10*

When the *mark of the beast* is established and enforced, the seventh-day Sabbath of God will take center stage.

What was the great sin of the *little horn power?* He spoke pompously against the Lord and thought to change God's "times and laws" (Dan 7:25). Scripture and history identify this power as the Papal system of the Roman Catholic Church. The Papacy thought they could change the Ten Commandment Law of God.

We have reviewed a number of their official documents that claim the act of changing Sabbath to Sunday was their mark of power and authority in religious matters. Here's one more for your consideration—

"Sunday is our mark of authority. The Church is above the Bible, and this transference of Sabbath observance is proof of the fact" (*The Catholic Record of London,* Ontario, Canada, September 1, 1923).

To grasp the end-time significance of this "mark of authority" claimed by the Catholic Church, we must first understand the *image of the beast* that will be set up on earth. Let's revisit Revelation 17:5—

"And on her forehead a name *was* written: MYSTERY, BABYLON THE GREAT, THE MOTHER OF HARLOTS AND OF THE ABOMINATIONS OF THE EARTH."

In Scripture, *woman* is used as a symbol to represent a community of God's people, a church. The true church is compared to a virtuous woman: "I have likened the daughter of Zion to a lovely and delicate woman" (Jer 6:2).

"For I am jealous for you with godly jealousy. For I have betrothed you to one husband, that I may present *you as* a chaste virgin to Christ" (2 Cor 11:2). In both Testaments, God called Himself the *husband* of the true church: "For your Maker *is* your husband, the LORD of hosts *is* His name" (Is 54:5).

When God's people apostatize, turning their backs on truth and the covenant terms of the Lord, the Bible compares them to a harlot committing fornication—

"I will punish her for the days of the Baals to which she burned incense. She decked herself with her earrings and jewelry, and went after her lovers; but Me she forgot," says the LORD" (Hos 2:13). "'Surely, *as* a wife treacherously departs from her husband, so have you dealt treacherously with Me, O house of Israel,' says the LORD" (Jer 3:20).

Scripture supplies the identifying marks for *mystery Babylon.* She is "the great harlot who sits on many waters" (Rev 17:1) and on seven mountains (vs. 9). The "kings of the earth committed fornication" with her (vs. 2). She is decked in purple and scarlet finery, and adorned with fine jewels (vs. 4). This great harlot was "drunk with the blood of the saints and with the blood of the martyrs of Jesus" (vs. 6).

In the early church, Christians commonly referred to Rome as *Babylon.* Horace, the Roman poet who died before Christ's birth, and the citizens of Rome described their city as "the city of seven hills." The pomp and wealthy circumstance of the Vatican has never succeeded in rewriting the history of her outrageous persecution of the saints.

The Protestant Reformers (and historicists today) identified this harlot with the *little horn power* and the *beast* of Revelation 13. They called the Roman Catholic Church "Mystery Babylon."

But if she is the "mother of harlots," who are her daughters? None are born harlots just because their mother is. To earn that distinction, they must choose to copy her ways. The daughters of mystery Babylon are other Christian churches who choose to follow her example. They imitate the image of their mother.

When the U.S. makes an "image of the beast," how will it breathe life into it—so that it speaks with authority? How will our government force all who dwell on the earth to receive a mark on their right hand or on their forehead, or suffer the consequences?

No one has received the mark of the beast yet. It will happen when the United States enforces Sunday-keeping laws, the mark of authority claimed by the Catholic Church.

In a time of extreme world crisis, our pseudo-Christian government—ignorant of God's Law—will think they can restore morality and God's favor by legislating Sunday laws. The Bible says they will exercise all the authority of the first beast (the Catholic Church) and will command all of humanity to worship on Sunday.

"He causes all, both small and great, rich and poor, free and slave, to receive a mark on their right hand or on their foreheads, and that no one may buy or sell except one who has the mark or the name of the beast, or the number of his name" (Rev 13:16-17) and "cause as many as would not worship the image of the beast to be killed" (vs. 15).

We have identified the symbolic meaning of *forehead* as referring to the "mind." But what is the symbolic interpretation of *hand?* In the Bible, *hand* is used to symbolize "actions."

Please consider these examples—

"Do not withhold good from those to whom it is due, when it is in the power of your hand to do *so*" (Prov 3:27). "But when you do a charitable deed, do not let your left hand know what your right hand is doing, that your charitable deed may be in secret; and your Father who sees in secret will Himself reward you openly" (Mt 6:3-4).

Because Revelation is filled with figurative language and symbols, *historicists* believe this mark does not represent a literal branding, but rather a support—by belief or by deeds—of the institution of the beast.

People will either believe the institution of Sunday-keeping to be good—receiving the *mark* in their *forehead* (mind), or in spite of their beliefs to the contrary, they will comply to avoid economic sanctions or death—receiving the *mark* in their *hand (actions)*.

Spiritual Babylon will birth many daughters. The Catholic Church will have their mark of authority, Sunday-keeping, spiritually tattooed in the minds or actions of the masses.

Satan will think he is the victor. That old dragon, the devil, desires to be as the Most High (Is 14:14). Satan's pride seeks for authority above God's authority. Pride motivated his rebellion and got him kicked out of heaven.

The conflict through the ages has been over worship. Satan tried to tempt Daniel and the three Hebrew worthies to worship his false system. When Christ endured the forty days of the desert temptation, the devil's greatest desire was to have Jesus worship him. Satan tried to coerce Christ by saying—

"All these things I will give You if You will fall down and worship me" (Mt 4:9).

Throughout the ages, Satan has sought the worship due to God. When his false day of worship is legislated throughout the world, he will think his antichrist agenda has succeeded. Satan will esteem himself exalted above the Most High, boasting triumphantly that he transformed the times and laws of God.

Yet God will always have a faithful remnant of people. "And the dragon was enraged with the woman, and he went to make war with the rest of her offspring, who keep the commandments of God and have the testimony of Jesus Christ" (Rev 12:17).

By threat or actual execution of death, Satan will seek to overcome the faithful. I know it seems absurd to us now, but the day will come when the ruling world power will pressure neighbors, friends, and even family members, to join in the persecution of the faithful for the good of the country. And the public will be persuaded by this philosophy.

Just consider the widespread reaction after the terrorist attack of September 11, 2001. The same citizens who had jealously guarded their liberties in the past were ready to relinquish certain rights without question. *Vigilante tactics*—normally abhorred by our free society—became acceptable standards to remove perceived enemies of the state. The victory of national *tolerance* gained over two centuries suffered an immediate blow.

A far more heinous example is the tragedy of the Holocaust. Nazi Germany prevailed over its citizens—some persuaded by national propaganda, others pressured by natural fear—to turn on innocent people. Historians estimate 5.6 to 5.9 million Jews were exterminated.

During the final climatic events before Christ returns, history will repeat itself. Jesus said, "… Yes, the time is coming that whoever kills you will think that he offers God service" (Jn 16:2).

Revelation identifies the people of God in this way: "Here is the patience of the saints; here *are* those who keep the commandments of God and the faith of Jesus" (Rev 14:12).

Recognizing the hour of His judgment has come, God's people will continue to give glory to Him, worshiping the Creator of heaven and earth (vs. 7). They will remember the loud call of the third angel—

"If anyone worships the beast and his image, and receives *his* mark on his forehead or on his hand, he himself shall also drink of the wine of the wrath of God, which is poured out full strength into the cup of His indignation. He shall be tormented with fire and brimstone in the presence of the holy angels and in the presence of the Lamb" (vs. 9-10)

Satan will not be the victor over God's faithful servants. "And they overcame him by the blood of the Lamb and by the word of their testimony, and they did not love their lives to the death" (Rev 12:11). They will not cast away their confidence in eternal life.

"Therefore do not cast away your confidence, which has great reward. For you have need of endurance, so that after you have done the will of God, you may receive the promise: 'For yet a little while, *and* He who is coming will come and will not tarry. Now the just shall live by faith; but if *anyone* draws back, My soul

has no pleasure in him.' But we are not of those who draw back to perdition, but of those who believe to the saving of the soul." *Hebrews 10:35-39*

If this is your first introduction to the *historicist* method of interpretation, I know this chapter could be unsettling. I don't believe in using scare tactics to bring people to God's truth. I hope you recognize the presentation of these facts have all come straight from Scripture.

Contemplating end-time events is a very sobering experience. But we don't have to be fearful. God promises us special grace to make it through this terrible time—and special grace at Christ's coming.

"And unless the Lord had shortened those days, no flesh would be saved; but for the elect's sake, whom He chose, He shortened the days" (Mk 13:20). "Therefore gird up the loins of your mind, be sober, and rest *your* hope fully upon the grace that is to be brought to you at the revelation of Jesus Christ" (1 Pet 1:13).

The message of the three angels of Revelation 14 is being broadcast throughout the world today. *Worship the true God of Creation, because the hour of God's judgment has come. Spiritual Babylon is fallen. Do not receive the mark of the beast.*

The voice from heaven is calling to God's people who are in the clutches of a system of spiritual confusion, "Come out of her, my people, lest you share in her sins, and lest you receive of her plagues" (Rev 18:4).

God is preparing His people for the Second Coming of Christ. He will preserve the faithful.

"Now may the God of peace Himself sanctify you completely; and may your whole spirit, soul, and body be preserved blameless at the coming of our Lord

Jesus Christ. He who calls you is faithful, who also will do it." *1 Thessalonians 5:23-24*

My faith is founded on the God Who sanctifies us and equips us for His purposes. This gives me great peace. And I'm eager to share the good news of chapter thirteen, *Resting in His Everlasting Arms.*

13

Resting In His Everlasting Arms

The eternal God is your refuge,
And underneath are the everlasting arms;
He will thrust out the enemy from before you,
And will say, 'Destroy!'
Deuteronomy 33:27

Sharing Scripture is always a joy for me. As serious students reflect on the Bible teachings examined in this book, I'm grateful when God opens their eyes to truth about the climax of time and Christ's Second Coming.

Still, for those releasing the error of the *secret rapture* and *left-behind* theories, self-doubt often drains the enthusiasm of discovery. Comments like this crop up: "I guess this means Christians will have to live through the tribulation. I'm not sure that I'm strong enough to face it."

The Bible chronicles a time of great tribulation before the Second Coming of Christ. Is it true Christians will have to face these closing trials? If so, how will we summon the strength to stand steadfast until the end?

Truth is critical. Our survival will depend on it. But you can breathe a deep sigh of relief—God has provided the answers. The greatest assurance we are offered is God's plan to prepare us and preserve us by His power.

One of the most insidious of Lucifer's lies is the sham of a *secret rapture* just before the tribulation and the mark of the beast. When the days of devastation descend, many sincere Christians will be caught ill-prepared.

Revelation warns that Satan will stage a counterfeit religious revival before Christ returns. With perverse pleasure, the devil will design spiritual delusions for the seduction of humanity. False miracles, signs, and wonders will be so spectacular that they create a snare for the sincere—but uninformed—Christian.

Many will accept the mark of the beast as the natural consequence of their spiritual apathy—they made no sincere effort to know the truths of God. That may sound like a harsh statement, but the Holy Spirit inspired Paul to record it—

"The coming of the *lawless one* is according to the working of Satan, with all power, signs, and lying wonders, and with all unrighteous deception among those who perish, because they did not receive the love of the truth, that they might be saved" (2 Thess 2:9-10).

Those who know and love the truth will dismiss the devil's delusions.

In Matthew 24, Jesus warns us to watch out for false prophets who will arise with great signs and wonders to deceive the very elect people of God, if possible. I submit to you that it *is possible.* Won't Christians who fail to learn Bible truths about end-time events and prophecies be at risk of Satan's great deceptions?

We have reviewed some of the prophecies. For a quick study of some signs of the end, I encourage you to read Matthew 24, Mark 13, Luke 21, and 2 Timothy 3.

Jesus warned that in the last days "lawlessness will abound"—*lawlessness* defined as breaking God's Ten Commandment Law—and "the love of many will grow cold" (Mt 24:12). In the end, disregard for the Law of Love (the Ten Commandments) will cause humanity's expression of God's love to evaporate.

Jesus identified the final sign of His coming when He said, "And this gospel of the kingdom will be preached in all the world as a witness to all the nations, and then the end will come" (Mt 24:14). Isn't it exciting to know that the gospel is now reaching every continent and nearly every nation of the world through satellite technology? Christians should rejoice. The end is near!

Will Christians have to endure to the end? According to Jesus, yes, we will. "… There will be great tribulation, such as has not been since the beginning of the world until this time, no, nor ever shall be. And unless those days were shortened, no flesh would be saved; but for the elect's sake those days will be shortened" (Mt 24:21-22).

Yet, those who know the truth and expect to experience the tribulation will not be downcast. In contrast to the masses, God's prepared people will lift their heads to the heavens, recognizing their redemption draws near. Jesus said—

"And there will be signs in the sun, in the moon, and in the stars; and on the earth distress of nations, with perplexity, the sea and the waves roaring; men's hearts failing them from fear and the expectation of those things which are coming on the earth, for the powers of heaven will be shaken. Then they will see the Son of Man coming in a cloud with power and great glory. Now when these things begin to happen, look up and lift up your heads, because your redemption draws near" (Lk 21:25-28).

Concerning the times and the seasons of the Second Coming, Paul warned that the arrival of Christ would be unexpected by most, just as a thief in the night appears unannounced to the unsuspecting homeowner (1 Thess 5:1-2). Comparing the climactic events to labor pains—increasing in intensity and frequency—Paul said—

"For when they say, 'Peace and safety!' then sudden

destruction comes upon them, as labor pains upon a pregnant woman. And they shall not escape" (vs. 3). Although no one knows the day or the hour of His coming (Mt 24:36), Paul writes that Christians who walk in the light of God's Word won't be caught off guard—

"But you, brethren, are not in darkness, so that this Day should overtake you as a thief. You are all sons of light and sons of the day. We are not of the night nor of darkness. Therefore ... let us watch and be sober. ... putting on the breastplate of faith and love, and as a helmet the hope of salvation. For God did not appoint us to wrath, but to obtain salvation through our Lord Jesus Christ, who died for us ..." (1 Thess 5:4-6, 8-10).

Consecrated Christians will recognize the signs of the times. Those who are abiding in an intimate relationship with Christ will be eagerly anticipating His return. Having accepted the gift of eternal life, we will rejoice at the thought of putting on immortality as the final victory over death (1 Cor 15:51-54).

Still, for those who suffer a superficial relationship with Christ, the Lord warns: "Be watchful, and strengthen the things which remain, that are ready to die, for I have not found your works perfect before God. Remember therefore how you have received and heard; hold fast and repent. Therefore if you will not watch, I will come upon you as a thief, and you will not know what hour I will come upon you" (Rev 3:2-3).

The Apostle Peter also wrote a sobering message about the end of times—a warning, mingled with a motivating message to persevere until the end. With the same clarion call, he echoes Christ's exhortation to be steadfast—

"But the day of the Lord will come as a thief in the night, in which the heavens will pass away with a great noise, and the elements will melt with fervent heat; both the earth and the works that are in it will be burned up. Therefore, since all these things will be dissolved, what manner of persons ought you to be in holy conduct and godliness, looking for and hastening the coming of the day … ?" (2 Pet 3:10-12).

Peter identifies another end-time sign: "… Scoffers will come in the last days, walking according to their own lusts, and saying, 'Where is the promise of His coming?...All things continue as they were from the beginning of creation'" (vs. 3-4).

He explains the error of these who jeer—they neglect the creative power of the Word of God.

In verses 5-7, Peter points out what they forget: 1) God created the world by the power of His Word; 2) He destroyed the world by commanding the fountains of the great deep to burst open and the floodgates of heaven to release a forty-day deluge of water; and 3) Our world today is now preserved by His same Word of power, and reserved for the coming firestorm.

Another alarm Peter sounded was to be cautious of unstable people who twist the Scriptures "to their own destruction" (vs. 16).

The hope of Peter's message is that the longsuffering of our Lord is our salvation (vs. 15). God is "not willing that any should perish but that all should come to repentance" (vs. 17). What is the Apostle's advice for survival?

"… Be diligent to be found by Him in peace, without spot and blameless … beware lest you also fall from your own steadfastness, being led away with the error of the wicked … but grow in the grace and knowledge of our Lord and Savior Jesus Christ …" (vss. 14, 17-18).

In this somewhat somber passage, Peter reminds us that God will recreate our earth once more—just as He did after the Great Flood. "Nevertheless we, according to His promise, look for new heavens and a new earth in which righteousness dwells" (vs. 13).

This is what motivates me to endure to the end! To think about spending a thousand years in heaven with my Lord, then to realize the Bible says heaven will come down to the new earth.

Can you envision this? You and I can spend eternity dwelling with God in the new earth that has been recreated in the splendor of the Garden of Eden. God will finally dwell with His family in whom He has perfected His image. Here's how John saw it in vision—

"Now I saw a new heaven and a new earth, for the first heaven and the first earth had passed away. Also there was no more sea. Then I, John, saw the holy city, New Jerusalem, coming down out of heaven from God ...

"And I heard a loud voice from heaven saying, 'Behold, the tabernacle of God is with men, and He will dwell with them, and they shall be His people. God Himself will be with them and be their God. And God will wipe away every tear from their eyes; there shall be no more death, nor sorrow, nor crying. There shall be no more pain, for the former things have passed away.'

"Then He who sat on the throne said, 'Behold, I make all things new. He who overcomes shall inherit all things, and I will be his God and he shall be My son. ... But the cowardly, unbelieving, abominable, murderers, sexually immoral, sorcerers, idolaters, and all liars shall have their part in the lake which burns with fire and brimstone, which is the second death'" (Rev 21:1-5, 7-8).

God offers all of humanity a choice between two alternatives—accept His gift of eternal life or perish. "For God so loved the world that He gave His only begotten Son, that whoever believes in Him should not perish but have everlasting life" (Jn 3:16).

Those who have rejected God's saving grace—either by choice or through apathetic neglect—will take part in the second resurrection (of the condemned) and receive the penalty of the second death. When their destruction is complete and God has made an end of sin, God promises that He will never let sin rise again (Nah 1:9).

Those who took part in the first resurrection will be in the glorious New Jerusalem when it descends to earth. And there will be more than enough space for the multitudes, for this is no ordinary-sized city.

"The city is laid out as a square; its length is as great as its breadth. And he measured the city with the reed: twelve thousand furlongs. Its length, breadth, and height are equal" (Rev 21:16). This is the "city four-square." It is actually a perfect cube, just as the Most Holy Place in the temple was shaped (1 Ki 6:20).

All of the city's measurements recorded in Revelation 21 are multiples of twelve, a number that is symbolic of God's people (twelve tribes in Israel, twelve apostles). This illustrates the New Jerusalem will be a perfect place to hold all of God's redeemed. If these dimensions were literal, the city would measure at least 344.6 miles on each side—approximately the size of the states of Oregon or Colorado.

The righteous will have a home in one of the mansions prepared by Christ in this capital city (Jn 14:2). Since the height of the city is equal to its length, I can envision some very tall mansions, can't you?

But there's more—we will have a country home in the new earth! When God described the glorious new creation to Isaiah, He explained that in the new earth we would build houses and inhabit them, plant gardens and eat the fruit of our labor, and enjoy the work of our hands (Is 65:21-22).

We won't be floating around on some fluffy cloud, strumming a harp. Clothed with immortality, we will have a real existence in the new earth in real bodies that resemble Christ's glorified body (Phi 3:21, Lk 24:39). Bodies that have abilities beyond Hollywood's imaginary bionic man!

Each week all the heirs of eternal life will gather in the New Jerusalem to spend the Sabbath day in the Presence of God (Is 66:23). We won't be confined to a temple building for our worship there, for John said—

"But I saw no temple in it, for the Lord God Almighty and the Lamb are its temple. The city had no need of the sun or of the moon to shine in it, for the glory of God illuminated it. The Lamb *is* its light" (Rev 21:22-23).

The Bible paints such a beautiful picture of what eternal life on the new earth will be. Still, haven't most Christians today lost sight of their inheritance? Few people realize that God will recreate the earth, because He *established* it forever (Ps 78:69).

God wants our understanding to be enlightened, that we may know "… what is the hope of His calling, what are the riches of the glory of His inheritance in the saints" (Eph 1:18). In the new earth, He will accomplish His original plan of perfection for all that He created.

If the lost and suffering people of this world only knew what a perfect Father our God is—if they only realized the inheritance He has planned as a gift—then they would be far more likely to accept the privilege of becoming His child. Can you think of someone who needs to know this?

I encourage you to share the good news with them. Jesus has commissioned us to "open their eyes, *in order* to turn *them* from darkness to light, and *from* the power of Satan to God, that they may receive forgiveness of sins and an inheritance among those who are sanctified by faith in Me" (Acts 26:18).

As the Apostle Paul went about strengthening the disciples, charging them to continue in the faith, he said, "We must through many tribulations enter the kingdom of God" (Acts 14:22).

He also encouraged the saints by saying, "For I consider that the sufferings of this present time are not worthy *to be compared* with the glory which shall be revealed in us" (Rom 8:18).

Yes, the people of God will face the great tribulation that

comes at the closing of the ages, but as we are "looking for the blessed hope and glorious appearing of our great God and Savior Jesus Christ" (Titus 2:13), we can count on God's power to become more than conquerors through it all.

"Who shall separate us from the love of Christ? *Shall* tribulation, or distress, or persecution, or famine, or nakedness, or peril, or sword? As it is written: 'For Your sake we are killed all day long; We are accounted as sheep for the slaughter.' Yet in all these things we are more than conquerors through Him who loved us.

"For I am persuaded that neither death nor life, nor angels nor principalities nor powers, nor things present nor things to come, nor height nor depth, nor any other created thing, shall be able to separate us from the love of God which is in Christ Jesus our Lord" (Rom 8:35-39).

God has a plan for us to overcome the trials and temptations of life here on earth—whether we are facing the common everyday battle, or the Great Tribulation. We don't have to live a defeated earthly existence.

We need to appreciate that once we have been born-again by His Word (1 Pet 1:23) and His Spirit (Jn 3:5), we must depend upon these two agencies for victory. God's Word is life to us! And God's plan is for us to depend totally upon Him and the power of His Spirit to walk in the footsteps of Christ.

For most of us, our problem is that we try to perfect our Christian walk by sheer human determination. Paul would say to us, "Are you so foolish? Having begun in the Spirit, are you now being made perfect by the flesh?" (Gal 3:3).

I'm excited to share the following, mostly paraphrased, Scripture promises that fortify my faith. These reassure me that I can face any trial as long as I totally depend on God. This is part of God's plan to take us through every fiery trial, up to the very day Christ returns.

God's Plan to Prepare Us and Preserve Us by His Power

1. God Expects Us to Rely on His Power.

Jesus said, "My grace is sufficient for you, for My power is made perfect in weakness" (2 Cor 12:9 NIV). He also said, "Without Me you can do nothing" (Jn 15:5). Our union to Christ is critical—we must rely on His power to work in us if we want to survive spiritually.

In John 15, Christ compared Himself to a vine and us to branches. We must live joined together with Him in an intimate relationship to have His power flow through us. A branch that is cut off from the vine can't thrive. Soon it withers and dies. In fact, the Lord described those who don't dwell in Him as deadwood, saying they will be gathered up with all the other dead branches and thrown into the burning fire (Jn 15:6).

Apart from Him, we can't accomplish anything of eternal consequence. But we can confidently claim, "I can do all things through Christ who strengthens me" (Phil 4:13). That's a promise God wants us to cling to every day of our lives.

2. God Provides Us with Transforming Power in His Word.

God's Word is filled with His creative power and does a life-changing work in believers (Heb 4:12; 1 Thess 2:13). As we trust in and apply His precious promises—putting His Word into practice—God releases His power in us and we actually become partakers of His divine character. This is our escape from the devil's clutches (2 Pe 1:3-4).

Jesus Christ upholds us by His mighty Word of power (Heb 1:3). If you want to experience a more intimate relationship with Jesus—the Living Word of God, develop a more intimate relationship with the Bible—the written Word of God.

3. **God Anoints Us with the Power of the Holy Spirit.**

"That He would grant you, according to the riches of His glory, to be strengthened with power through His Spirit in the inner man ... Now to Him who is able to do far more abundantly beyond all that we ask or think, according to the power that works within us, to Him *be* the glory ..." (Eph 3:16, 20-21 NASB).

When we were born-again, God claimed us as children and stamped us with His seal of approval when He anointed us with the Holy Spirit as a pledge—much as we apply our signature to a real estate contract and offer "earnest money." This anointing affirms we belong to Him and is the power that produces perseverance in Christ (2 Cor 1:21-22).

As the anointing of the Holy Spirit abides in us, He teaches us all truth (1 Jn 2:27). God's Word is spiritual and spiritually discerned (1 Cor 2:14). True understanding comes as we walk in obedience, keeping in step with the Spirit (Gal 5:25). Only those who are led by the Spirit of God are really the children of God (Rom 8:14). The greater our obedience, the greater supply of the Spirit we receive from our Lord (Acts 5:32).

4. **God Issues Us Spiritual Weapons.**

There is a world war going on right now. It's between the devil's destructive forces of darkness and evil, and the Lord's creative power of light and purity. The greatest war we wage is in our minds!

God knows we can't confront the spiritual struggle using human methods, so He supplies spiritual weapons of divine power. With these we squash speculations that oppose His truths, shatter strongholds of the devil, and seize our thoughts—making them obedient to Christ (2 Cor 10:3-5). We are instructed to "take up the whole armor of God, that you may be able to withstand in the evil day, and having done all, to stand" (Eph 6:13).

Our armor includes: a) The belt of truth—reliability of God's Word; b) the breastplate of righteousness—Christ's righteousness credited to us; c) Gospel shoes—secure footing on the foundation of Christ; d) the shield of faith—in God's character, Word and power; e) the helmet of salvation—blessed assurance in God's gift; f) the sword of the Spirit—the Word of God; and g) the power of prayer—granting God permission to intervene and release His power into all situations. Put this armor on and you will stand firm in faith (Eph 6:14-18).

5. God Guides Us and Delivers from Evil.

All of humanity faces the same temptations, but God won't let us be tempted beyond our strength to resist it. We can count on Him to provide the escape route from evil (1 Cor 10:13). To preserve us, God will deliver us from every evil and bring us safely into His heavenly kingdom (2 Tim 4:18). The Lord will guide us by His Word and afterward receive us to glory (Ps 73:24).

God is our "hiding place"—He preserves us from trouble and surrounds us with songs of deliverance (Ps 32:7). "He who dwells in the secret place of the Most High shall abide under the shadow of the Almighty" (Ps 91:1).

6. Christ Constantly Intercedes for Us.

Before His crucifixion, Jesus warned Peter that a time of testing was coming—Satan would try to separate him from the Lord, like chaff from wheat. Then Christ encouraged him by saying, "But I have prayed for you, that your faith should not fail; and when you have returned to *Me*, strengthen your brethren" (Lk 22:31-32).

You and I need to be aware of the devil's devious ways, intended to separate us from God. But we can take comfort in knowing that Christ continually intercedes for us, as our high Priest: "Therefore He is able also to save forever, those who draw near to God through Him, since He always lives to make intercession for them" (Heb 7:25 NASB).

7. God Never Forsakes Those Who Draw Near to Him.

With a passionate heart, God works to woo us to His infinite love through His Spirit and His Word. God promises that if we draw near to Him, He will draw near to us. As we commit and submit our lives to God, He gives us the power to resist evil—and the devil must flee from us (Ja 4:7-8).

In God's great mercy He assures us, "I will never leave you nor forsake you." With extreme confidence we can say, "The LORD *is* my helper; I will not fear. What can man do to me?" (Heb 13:5-6).

Christ said that His followers would flee from the voice of a stranger. He promised we would hear His voice and follow Him only (Jn 10:5, 27). "And I give them eternal life, and they shall never perish; neither shall anyone snatch them out of My hand. My Father, who has given *them* to Me, is greater than all; and no one is able to snatch *them* out of My Father's hand" (Jn 10:28-29).

8. God Completes His Work of Perfection in Us.

We have a hope and a destiny! If we love God and accept His plan for our lives, this is our hope—He will work out everything that happens to us in life for our eternal benefit! And this is our destiny—God's plan for us who accept Christ as Savior is to shape our character into His image (Rom 8:28-29).

Through His Word and His Spirit, God works in us to cause us to desire His will and to empower us to act in a way that pleases Him (Phil 2:13). We can be confident that "… He who has begun a good work in you will complete *it* until the day of Jesus Christ" (Phil 1:6). Through the blood of the eternal covenant, God will "make you complete in every good work to do His will, working in you what is well pleasing in His sight, through Jesus Christ …" (Heb 13:20-21). Hallelujah!

9. God Keeps Us Blameless.

By God's grace, we are enriched in every way in Christ as we eagerly wait for His return. In faithfulness, He will confirm us to the very end so that we may stand blameless—free from sin and guilt—in the day of our Lord Jesus Christ (1 Cor 1:4-9).

The Lord will cause us to increase in love, so that He can establish us in holiness, keeping us blameless before God at the Second Coming of Christ (1 Thess 3:12-13). God will keep us by His power. He will not allow our foot to slip—He will preserve us from all evil (Ps 121:2-7).

We need to be like Abraham, who accepted God's Word and was fully convinced that God had the power to perform all that He promised (Rom 4:20-22). We need to be like Paul, who was persuaded that God was able to protect him and keep all that he had entrusted to Him until Christ's return (2 Tim 1:12).

10. God Fights the Battle and Gives Us the Victory!

Our struggle is not against "flesh and blood" people, but against Satan and his unholy alliance (Eph 6:12).

God knows that without Him, we are no match against these forces of evil. He claims the battle belongs to Him (1 Sam 17:47). He gives us the victory through Christ (1 Cor 15:57). We don't need to be fearful. God is the One Who goes with us into our battles and He will not leave us or forsake us (Deut 31:6).

"... Fear not, for I have redeemed you; I have called *you* by your name; You *are* Mine. When you pass through the waters, I *will be* with you; and through the rivers, they shall not overflow you. When you walk through the fire, you shall not be burned, nor shall the flame scorch you. For I *am* the LORD your God, the Holy One of Israel, your Savior ..." (Is 43:1-3).

Grace grants us total dependence on God to perfect everything that concerns our salvation. In fact, as we have just reviewed, God vows to perform His perfection in us if we remain in Him.

Still, His grace does not excuse disobedience. Rather, grace empowers us to obey the Law of God. In His love, the Lord only requires of us what He will equip us to do.

The natural man is born governed by a *rule of action* that holds our sin nature captive—*the law of sin and death* (Rom 7:23, 25). But Christ delivers us from our natural tendencies when we accept Him as our personal Savior.

To recreate us, He breathes new life into our beings. The life force He imparts introduces a new *rule of action* to regulate our thoughts and behavior. Paul defined it as the *law of the Spirit of Life.*

By the indwelling Spirit of Christ's life, we are imbued with power—power to perceive God's will, overcome sin, obey, and persevere. "For the law of the Spirit of life in Christ Jesus has made me free from the law of sin and death" (Rom 8:2).

Our part in the plan of salvation is to accept God's Word by faith, and turn our faith into actions. "Faith by itself, if it does not have works, is dead" (Ja 2:17). The Apostle John warned us not to be deceived—only those who *practice* righteousness are righteous like Christ (1 Jn 3:7).

Christ didn't obey *to become* God's Son—He obeyed because He *was* the holy Son of God. In like manner, we don't obey *to be* saved—we obey because we *are* saved. The entrance of God's Word brings light and understanding to our lowly minds—the Word is a light to show us His path of life (Ps 119:130, 105; Ps 16:11).

"If we walk in the light as He is in the light, we have fellowship with one another, and the blood of Jesus Christ His Son cleanses us from all sin" (1 Jn 1:7). To walk in the light means to walk in obedience to His Word. Obedience keeps us in the light, just as Christ is in the light. In fact, the Bible says obedience leads to righteousness (Rom 6:16).

"If you love Me, keep My commandments" (Jn 14:15). Obedience is the highest expression of worship. God's end-time people will obey all of His Ten Commandments—including His seventh-day (Saturday) Sabbath.

Yes, the Great Tribulation will bring persecution upon those who remain loyal to God's true system of worship and refuse the mark of the beast. Still, God will exchange His strength for ours, providing us the power to persevere.

And just as He protected the Israelites when He visited the plagues upon Egypt, He will shield us from the seven last deadly plagues (Rev 15:1-16:21) prior to delivering us from bondage.

The world may persecute Christ's faithful followers, but Almighty God protects His obedient children. And the very first moment of eternity—when we see our Savior face-to-face—will be worth every trial we faced on this old earth.

"Here is the patience of the saints; here *are* those who keep the commandments of God and the faith of Jesus" (Rev 14:12).

Just like King David of the Old Testament, our "times" are

in God's hand. In God's great mercy, He will make His face to shine upon the faithful. As we call upon the Lord, He will not allow us to be put to shame—

"Oh, love the LORD, all you His saints! *For* the LORD preserves the faithful … Be of good courage, and He shall strengthen your heart, all you who hope in the LORD" (Ps 31:23-24).

As we step out in faith to keep God's commandments, God keeps us by His perfect power. The power of the Holy Spirit is behind our every action of obedience. Obedience keeps us abiding in Christ and He holds us in His Hand—close to His heart.

The eternal God is our refuge and we are safe, surrounded by His love, resting in His everlasting arms.

14

Celebrating Our Sanctification

Have you ever wondered, "How can I know God's will?" Pressed for an answer that was straight to the point, I turned to the Bible and discovered "This is the will of God, your sanctification" (1 Thess 4:3).

But, what does that mean for me in my everyday life?

Sanctification. If this is God's will for us, don't you think it's critical that we fully comprehend its meaning? What is it? How do we obtain it? How will we know when we are experiencing it? What does the Sabbath have to do with it?

Christians often toss the word "sanctification" around in conversation, while suffering from a vague understanding of what it spells out for their lives.

To be *sanctified* means to be "set apart" for the glory of God—set apart from worldly things and wicked actions. The synonym for *sanctification* is "holiness." To be *sanctified* means to be *made holy.*

When the Holy Spirit of God—the Spirit of holiness—is living in us and leading us, we can be confident that God is working in us to cause the actions of our personal conduct to conform to the holiness of His Son.

In fact, the Apostle Peter tells us that because our Heavenly Father is holy, we—His children—are to be holy in *all* our conduct. God doesn't want us to suffer the consequences of sin, so He lovingly instructs us, "Be holy, for I am holy" (1 Pet 1:15-16).

Does the subject of holiness make you uneasy? Perhaps it's because you are familiar with what man has labeled *holiness movements* in the church. These generally spring forth from a sincere desire to draw closer to God, but so many holiness movements have marred His reputation.

It's easy to understand why. Man focuses on the outward appearance of things, and concocts rules to constrain the conduct of people to a limited *human perception* of holiness. Sadly, the result is often nothing more than cold legalism, empty talk, and hypocrisy.

This external philosophy fooled the Pharisees. They became vain, self-righteous, judgmental, and two-faced. With a religious swagger, they walked with a "holier than thou" attitude.

Jesus labeled them as frauds and compared them to "whitewashed tombs" (Mt 23:27). On the outside they *appeared* to be all cleaned up—on the inside they were rotting. True holiness is rooted in humility, having the same humble mind of our Lord and Savior, Jesus Christ (Phil 2:5-8).

In contrast to outward appearances, God looks at the heart (1 Sam 16:7). And human effort alone can't produce *heart* holiness. The very best effort we can put forth is to *surrender* control of our lives to God.

We must allow Him to work out His will in us as He unites us with Christ. Holiness is a fruit that grows only from our union with Christ.

As we live in the reality of *redemption in Christ*, God pours His love and power into us through His Spirit. In other words, God empowers us to respond to Him in holy righteousness—*right doing.* When we have a personal relationship with Christ, we are no longer powerless over sin.

As Paul said, we must recognize that we have "been set free from sin, and ... have ... fruit [attitudes and actions developed] to holiness, and the end, everlasting life" (Rom 6:22).

Most of us are familiar with the doctrine of *righteousness by faith.* I have good news. Sanctification comes by faith, too! Sanctification is God's work in us that makes us righteous!

It is God Who has set us apart from evil. It is God Who is working in us to make us holy. As we cooperate with Christ, He imparts His life to us and converts us into His image. In fact, Paul said that Christ *in us* is our only "hope of glory" (Col 1:27).

Contrary to the vanity of many so-called *holiness movements,* the life of Christ cleanses us from the inside out. As His work is accomplished in us, we are empowered to walk in His holy footsteps.

The Bible spells out our dependence upon God to become holy—

- Christ is our sanctification (1 Cor 1:30).
- We have been sanctified through Christ offering His body—once for all (Heb 10:10).
- We are sanctified by the blood of Christ, the eternal covenant (Heb 10:29, 13:12).
- We are sanctified by faith in Christ (Acts 26:18).
- We are sanctified by God the Father, and preserved in Jesus Christ (1 Thess 5:23; Jude 1:1).
- We are sanctified by God's truth, the Holy Bible (Jn 17:17; Eph 5:26).
- We are sanctified by the Holy Spirit (2 Thess 2:13; 1 Cor 6:11).
- We are sanctified by the Spirit for the purpose of obedience (1 Pe 1:2).

Whoops, there's that word again—obedience. Yes, we play a cooperative part in developing holiness. Paul said that our part is to abandon sinful behavior to become "a vessel for honor, sanctified and useful for the Master, prepared for every good work" (2 Tim 2:21). He explained obedience leads to righteousness (Rom 6:16).

With Christ as our Teacher, our minds will be renewed. We will discard our former conduct and, as Paul insists, *put on* our new nature "which was created according to God, in true righteousness and holiness" (Eph 4:20-24).

I love the balance Paul brings to his writings. On the one hand, he extends the promise of God to do a sanctifying work in us. On the other hand, he encourages us to do our part to cooperate with God.

Sanctification is not just some *thing* that God does in us—it is the very life of Christ working in us. *Holiness* is what we *are* when dedicated wholly to the Lord. It is a condition God creates in us when we accept His rule in our lives and choose to follow Christ without reservation.

In practical, everyday actions, we must *work out* the life He has placed inside of us. This is a struggle that makes us grow and increases our strength.

Paul said, "Work out your own salvation with fear and trembling." But he admonishes us not to try this in our own strength, for he says, "It is God who works in you both to will and to do for *His* good pleasure" (Phil 2:12-13).

"He who is joined to the Lord is one spirit *with Him*" (1 Cor 6:17). Isn't that a beautiful promise of what God will accomplish in our lives? Through sanctification, the character of Christ is created in us.

As He imparts His holiness, He makes us one with Him. The effect is obedience, which occurs naturally, once we have made the decision to follow Him and have dedicated our lives to His cause—whatever the cost.

Prayer and Bible study are the way we communicate with our Lord. If our choice is clear and our love "for real," communication will occur quite spontaneously once we have been taught how.

So we are admonished, "Pursue ... holiness, without which no one will see the Lord: looking carefully lest anyone fall short of the grace of God ..." (Heb 12:14-15). As we pursue holiness, we are fully persuaded that sanctification is God's work—a work we should celebrate!

God intended the Sabbath to be a celebration of our sanctification. "Surely My Sabbaths you shall keep, for it *is* a sign between Me and you throughout your generations, that *you* may know that I *am* the LORD who sanctifies you" (Ex 31:13).

Sabbath-keeping deepens our experience of sanctification—of being set apart for the glory of God. It helps us to *work out* His sanctifying power into a deliberate devotion to our Lord and His interests.

As we reflect on His infinite love, God restores the joy of our salvation. Particularly as we recall it is God Who is working in us to make us holy! We remember we are worth nothing less than the price He paid for us, with the precious blood of Jesus. The result is an abiding appreciation of His grace and the love He lavished on us through His Calvary Plan.

The object of the Sabbath is "oneness" with God—a day when we wholeheartedly concentrate on our relationship with Him. God wants us to call His holy day a delight, not a day of drudgery (Is 58:13).

In our time-starved world, we can become disjointed from relationships that should be our top priority. The Sabbath is a gift of time—a time for perfect reunion with God and family—a "time out" that restores and sustains our peace and joy.

Didn't Jesus say, in the literal Greek translation of Mark 2:27, that He made the Sabbath for "the sake of mankind"? This is our God-given holiday from the hassles of everyday life. On this special day, we can ignore worldly demands and enter a time of refreshing from the Lord. God rejuvenates us spiritually and physically.

Our world is sullied by sin—spinning out of control. And, our *spiritual vision* becomes blurred from time to time, doesn't it? The Sabbath is God's solution to woo us away from the world and refocus our fragmented attention. For one full day, we set aside individual worldly interests and we seek our pleasure in Him.

The Lord designed this day to be a memorial of His love, His sovereign power, and our true rest, found in Christ alone. Can you see God's divine plan in this? As we celebrate His goodness, it results in a weekly recommitment to seek first His kingdom and His righteousness (Mt 6:33).

"Do you not know that your body is the temple of the Holy Spirit *who is* in you, whom you have from God, and you are not your own? For you were bought at a price; therefore glorify God in your body and in your spirit, which are God's" (1 Cor 6:19-20).

The Sabbath is a weekly reminder that Christ paid the price to purchase our freedom from the bondage of sin. We belong to Him. He wants to have an intimate relationship with us. He sanctified the Sabbath hours for us to celebrate His love, worship Him, and enjoy Christian fellowship with family and friends.

Still, the spirit of Sabbath-keeping is more than a time of worship, fellowship, and physical rest. It's also a time that we can use to work side-by-side with the Savior, performing acts of mercy and Christian service. Jesus said, "Therefore it is lawful to do good on the Sabbath" (Mt 12:12).

God did not intend for us to observe a "stop and go" Sabbath. It's wrong to merely screech to a *stop* at the signal of the Sabbath, sit idly by in boredom, and then rev up our engines to *go* again as soon as the weekday signal comes on.

If we do not celebrate the spirit of the Sabbath, we will become legalistic in our observance and present a pitiful picture of God to our family and friends. Rules without relationship result in rebellion!

So how do we celebrate the Sabbath in such a way that it becomes a day of happiness and holy joy? There is no perfect model that must be followed. Our Sabbath celebration should be flexible to meet our personal spiritual and physical needs.

But it would be wrong to bring you this far in exposing the Sabbath truth without sharing suggestions to stimulate your own enthusiastic devotion to God's holy day.

I'm not an expert, and my suggestions are by no means all-inclusive. Still, if you are new to the concept of *celebrating* the Sabbath—which even many Sabbath-*keepers* are—the following ideas may be of benefit to you.

These suggestions are addressed to families. If you're single, apply them to a gathering of friends. If you are the only member of the family who has accepted the Sabbath truth, do all you can to implement these practices and allow God to show your family His holy day is full of joy. If your actions demonstrate that the Sabbath is a time of delight, then family members will be more likely to join you in this day of perfect harmony with the Lord.

How to Celebrate the Sabbath

1. **Preparation throughout the week.** As we experience the joy of the Sabbath, something interesting happens. We develop an attitude of valuing God's day as the most important day of our week.

   Soon we find we are arranging the entire week around the Sabbath, rather than scheduling all of our preparations for Friday—the "Preparation Day" designated by Scripture. This allows us to enter the

Sabbath less stressed. Once Sabbath-keeping becomes a rhythm of relationship with God, we benefit from better organization of *all* our weekly activities.

The Sabbath is not a day for commercial commotion. God instructs us not to be distracted with buying and selling (Jer 17:27; Neh 10:31, 13:15-22). This requires advanced planning of meals and major chores.

To keep Friday's preparation to a minimum, it's helpful to complete grocery shopping, laundry, and major housekeeping early in the week. Also, you might consider filling your car with fuel on Thursday.

2. **Friday—Preparation Day.** Sabbath is Mother's day to be relieved of slaving in the kitchen. Keep menus simple, or do the major portion of production in advance, so that Sabbath meals need only to be warmed and served.

Don't become legalistic by being overly restrictive regarding food preparation. The disciples plucked grain from the fields on the Sabbath (Mk 12:1). It was not a major harvest job. They were just meeting their physical needs, and Jesus approved their actions.

Tidy up the house so that the Sabbath-rest can be enjoyed in a neat environment. Perhaps you could set the table in a special way—adorning it with flowers, making this a night for candles at your dinner setting. Do something to make special memories and instill a fondness in your children for the joy of God's holy day.

Try copying Scripture promises, to be hidden under place settings. At the end of the meal, each family member will have a treat from the Word of God. Turn on inspirational music an hour in advance to prepare your hearts for the occasion.

3. **Friday—Sunset.** God's system of time keeping is from sunset to sunset (Gen 1:2) and He applied this to the Sabbath (Lev 23:32). God had a definite purpose in this and it is the preferred manner of Sabbath observance. When we start our celebration on Friday evening, our rest is increased and our hearts are prepared for worship on Saturday.

Create Sabbath traditions in your home. To enhance the special atmosphere of welcoming the Sabbath, light candles and welcome Jesus, the "light of the world" (Jn 8:12). Start the Sabbath with a special song. Rehearse what the day represents, recognizing God as Creator, Redeemer, Savior, and the One Who sanctifies. Have a short family prayer, welcoming God's special visitation to your home.

Is there a favorite meal your family enjoys? Mexican, Italian, American, a specialty salad, or a hearty vegetable stew? Make it your tradition to have this on Friday evening. For easy cleanup afterward, you could use fancy paper plates, or use dishware that can be easily rinsed and stacked.

There's no perfect formula for opening the Sabbath—create traditions of your own.

Just make the meal enjoyable, with conversation focusing around testimonies of what the Lord has done over the past week.

If Scripture promises have been hidden under the place settings, encourage each family member to share their promise aloud and then to claim it every day until the next Sabbath. This will help to hide God's Word in their heart.

After dinner, the family could take a walk to stargaze. If you have a telescope, identify the stars and talk about God's Creation. Or, have a family songfest.

Friday evening is a good time to review and discuss Bible lessons before church.

Whatever you do, try to involve all family members. Families are falling apart because they have so little quality time with each other. Children will come to welcome the Sabbath with joy if they see it *is* a time of joy. Have a short prayer before the family retires for bed.

4. **Sabbath Morning.** Make Sabbath mornings special with family favorites for breakfast. Get up early enough to avoid a frenzied rush before leaving for church. After breakfast, have a short devotional to prepare hearts and minds for worship at church. God set aside Sabbath time for "a holy convocation" (Lev 23:3).

Load the family into your automobile with Bibles, lessons and notepads—and don't forget to grab the casseroles if you will be staying for church fellowship dinner. Make the ride to church a pleasant time, singing songs or rehearsing Bible promises. Please don't shipwreck the Sabbath by fussing on the way to church.

Sabbath-school is designed to delight youngsters, but young children sometimes have difficulty sitting quietly through the church service. Try giving them a notebook and have them write down keywords the speaker uses, such as *God, Jesus, grace, love.* Each time the word is mentioned, have them make a mark after it.

They will listen attentively throughout the sermon, and at the conclusion they can count the number of times each word was used. God's Word can penetrate hearts through listening ears—no matter how young they are. For good behavior, promise a special treat after lunch as a reward.

5. **Sabbath Afternoon.** What will you do for Sabbath lunch? Are you staying for a fellowship dinner at church? Will the family go home and heat up a prepared meal? Have you invited friends to join you? Is the weather right for a picnic? Whatever you do, make the children feel a special part of the activities, always reminding them that this is a day dedicated to celebrating God glory.

Now, what can you do on Sabbath afternoons? A lot! Sabbath celebration is intended to draw us closer to God, and to our loved ones. It is a time of peace, when we can shut out the daily problems of the world.

God reserved one day a week for our rest and for the joy of communing with Him. It's more than a day for church services—it's a day to develop a deepening personal relationship with our Creator God. Here are a few suggestions:

- Celebrate God's Creation—Take a nature walk, a country drive, go bird watching, or rowing on the lake, seeing God's handiwork in every detail of nature. Keep the conversation focused on God. Take a camera along, collect flowers, insects, or other objects of nature and start a Creation scrapbook.
- Celebrate God's Gift of Music—Gather around the piano or get out the guitar and have a songfest, learn a new Christian song, or write a song about the Lord.
- Celebrate God's Mercy—Do something to relieve the suffering of others. Visit shut-ins or orphanages, write cards of encouragement to those who are ill or grieving, feed the homeless. Create craftwork to take to shut-ins.
- Celebrate God's Word—Share a Bible story or

Scripture promises. Let the children reenact a Bible story or have a Bible treasure hunt. Allow them to lead in a family devotional. Play Bible games. Give a friend a Bible study.

- Celebrate God's Rest—Take a nap! Read the Bible or a good Christian book.
- Celebrate Prayer—Write out your prayer to the Lord in a prayer journal. Or start a family journal of dated prayer requests and dated answers.
- Celebrate the Family—Focus on deepening your relationship with each other and with God. Discuss God's plan for each family member, how you can draw nearer to Him, and how to recognize His leading. Talk about God's loving character, and how He is recreating each of you to be transformed into His divine nature.
- Celebrate the Hope of Eternal Life—Talk about eternal life in the new earth. Encourage children to imagine building a country home out of living materials, riding on a tiger's back, or playing with some other animal that will no longer be threatening.

6. **Coming to the Sabbath's end.** Try making the final meal light and fun! Perhaps you could pop popcorn and serve a variety of fruits, along with favorite appetizers.

As the sun begins to set, close the Sabbath with testimonies of thanksgiving and another short prayer. Recommit to live for God's glory and ask the Lord to make His power perfect in your weakness—to exchange His strength for yours—through the upcoming week.

Can you see how the Sabbath is designed to deepen our love relationship with God? How could we help but celebrate as we focus on His creative power and recognize that same power is at work within us?

As we draw near to Him, He draws near to us (Ja 4:8), and then He works to draw families closer together. Our Redeemer restores us through His special day of rest.

On the sixth day of Creation, can you imagine the angels watching with eager expectation and wondering what God would create next to prove the wonders of His love?

Think about the rejoicing there must have been in heaven when, on the seventh day of Creation, the Creator said His unique work was done—and declared it to be good!

God rested from His work, not because He was weary, but because He was well pleased.

He crowned His creation with a day set aside to commemorate His glorious act of love. He ordained the seventh day for the benefit of man—for our spiritual and physical health—so we could respond to His love.

God sanctified this sacred day for eternity as a perpetual covenant (Ex 31:16). He called it "My holy day" (Is 58:13). Sabbaths are to celebrate our relationship with God—a sign of His covenant to sanctify us.

The "antichrist agenda" is to rob us of this intimate relationship. The devil desires to deceive us into paying homage to him, thereby destroying our loyalty to God.

Hear the special messengers a loving God has sent to warn us with a loud voice, "Fear God and give glory to Him, for the hour of His judgment has come; and worship Him who made heaven and earth, the sea and springs of water … Babylon is fallen, is fallen, that great city, because she has made all nations drink of the wine of the wrath of her fornication. …

"If anyone worships the beast and his image, and receives *his* mark on his forehead or on his hand, he himself shall also drink of the wine of the wrath of God, which is poured out full strength into the cup of His indignation …" (Rev 14:7-10).

Just as in Isaiah 30:15, the voice of the heavenly Father is still calling, "In returning and rest you shall be saved; in quietness and confidence shall be your strength." That beautiful promise reflects the spirit of the Sabbath.

But sadly, the Scripture does not end there. The heartbreak of God's disappointment can be sensed as He adds, "But you would not."

Can a child of God, led by the Holy Spirit, ignore the only commandment that God emphasized we should *remember*—the seventh-day (Saturday) Sabbath?

Listen to the voice of our loving Savior calling out to us now, "If you love Me, keep My commandments" (Jn 14:15).

For this is the love of God, that we keep His commandments. And His commandments are not burdensome. For whatever is born of God overcomes the world. And this is the victory that has overcome the world—our faith. *1 John 5:3-4*

By faith, we can overcome the world's system of false religion. By faith, we can abolish the manipulative mind-control of the "antichrist agenda" and accept the victory God wants to give us through our Lord Jesus.

Christ's power *living in us* creates the momentum to keep God's commandments. Our love for Him creates the motive.

"Now to Him who is able to keep you from stumbling, and to present you faultless before the presence of His glory with exceeding joy, to God our Savior, Who alone is wise, be glory and majesty, dominion and power, both now and forever." *Jude 1:24-25*

Amen.

Epilogue

If, after examining the Scriptures of this study, you think I'm *off the mark* for being a seventh-day Sabbath celebrator, I would welcome any Bible evidence you can share. If you know Scriptures that are contrary to what I hold dear as truth, then please love me enough to show me.

I've studied this subject for many years, desiring only the truth. I have diligently looked into the Fourth Commandment, which tells us to keep the Sabbath holy, frequently reexamining the original Hebrew and Greek. As many Bible scholars before me, I cannot find any scriptural evidence of authority to change the day God calls "My holy day."

I've examined every Scripture people have thrown at me to invalidate the Fourth Commandment, comparing it with the Greek or Hebrew. What I have discovered in every instance is that God's Ten Commandment Law has always been in effect and will continue to be in effect throughout the eons of eternity.

May God continue to bless each of us as we press forward in our quest for a better understanding of His wonderful and amazing character of love.

Danny Shelton

For a more detailed study of end-time events and Bible prophecies, please write Three Angels Broadcasting Network at: P.O. Box 220, West Frankfort, IL 62896, or call (618) 627-4651. These studies can also be accessed on the web at: www.3abn.org, www.vop.com, or www.amazingfacts.org.

About the Authors

Danny Shelton is founder and President of Three Angels Broadcasting Network (3ABN), a 24-hour Christian television and radio network. In 1984, Danny was impressed to build a television station that would reach the world with the undiluted truth of the Gospel. Today—with production centers in Southern Illinois and Nizhny Novgorod, Russia—3ABN beams its signal to every inhabited continent on earth, with a potential viewing audience of several hundred million souls. Danny has authored three international best-sellers with sales of nearly three million copies.

Shelley Quinn is Speaker and Co-Director for Word Warrior Ministries. As a Christian author and Bible teacher, she travels the United States and abroad preaching the Gospel of Christ at revivals, retreats and camp meetings. Shelley hosts *Exalting His Word* on 3ABN's television and radio networks, with a strong focus on the transforming power of God's Word and His Spirit.